T0357019

Dancing
on My
Own
Two Feet

Dancing on My Own Two Feet

A New Life
One Step at a Time

Jenn Todling

SHE WRITES PRESS

Published 2025

Printed in the United States of America

Print ISBN: 978-1-64742-878-5
E-ISBN: 978-1-64742-879-2
Library of Congress Control Number: 2024925806

For information, address:
She Writes Press
1569 Solano Ave #546
Berkeley, CA 94707

Interior design and typeset by Katherine Lloyd, The DESK

She Writes Press is a division of SparkPoint Studio, LLC.

Names and identifying characteristics have been changed
to protect the privacy of certain individuals.

For my guardian angel, Uncle Tom:
Thank you for being one of my biggest cheerleaders
who fully embraced living life on your own terms.
Cheers to a thousand purple books in your memory.

Author's Note

This book is a memoir. Except for the names of my siblings, other names and some identifying characteristics have been changed, some events have been compressed, and some dialogue has been recreated. Any resemblance between fictionalized content and any real person is strictly coincidental.

Prologue

It was Saturday morning, and my eyes were glued to the TV. *Star Search* had just come on, and Ed McMahon was getting ready to announce the next dance act to perform. Two ten-year-olds stood at center stage as the volume of the pulsating background music increased. A mesmerizing techno beat played as the duo twisted and turned, shifting between upbeat jazz moves and tumbling gymnastics as they moved across the dance floor. I took copious mental notes, figuring out which moves I wanted to replicate in my weekly dance practice with my younger sister and her two neighborhood friends. The gymnastics moves were a little advanced, but I figured I could work up to that by helping my dance trio learn back walkovers, with some spotting from me, and add a few cartwheels to supplement our dance repertoire. I stood next to the TV and imitated the dance moves, the teal-green shag carpet in my living room making it difficult to move. Unbothered, I practiced the moves one after another until I felt them etched into my body. I could feel the rhythm and beat within me, and I couldn't wait to incorporate the dance steps into my choreography. Without a care in the world, I was in the zone, focused solely on personal expression.

"Jennifer, we're here," my eight-year-old sister, Rose, yelled from the bottom of the stairs in our tri-level home. She had just arrived with her two best friends. They giggled as they ran up the staircase and into the living room to join me.

"Guess what, guys! I just learned some amazing new moves! I

can't wait to try them out." I shut off the TV as the credits rolled, placed a battered CD into the tray table, and pressed play. It was Madonna, the queen of the '90s.

"Let's warm up to 'Holiday,'" I offered as we started jumping back and forth, imitating the pony dance, a dance my mom had taught me in my early childhood days.

We smiled as we ran around the living room, did jumping jacks, and turned from side to side as we prepared to stretch our bodies to the max. It was just the four of us in the house that day. My dad was working at the local grocery store, something he did every weekend. My eleven-year-old brother, Richard, was at a friend's house, and my mom was getting settled in her new apartment. We were all still adjusting to my parents' divorce.

My siblings and I were used to being alone and finding ways to create our own sense of adventure at our modest home on the outskirts of Boulder, Colorado. As the oldest, I was in charge. During my Saturday dance rehearsals, I didn't mind the added responsibility. I was in my happy place. I didn't care that I was self-taught and didn't have any professional dance training to date. The creative expression fueled me, and I enjoyed taking a break from caring for my younger siblings. When I was dancing, I felt in control and centered. I was in tune with my needs, and I did my best to honor them. Dancing brought me balance and peace.

My mom surprised me with a special outing to Springers Night-club, a dive just outside of Boulder, to celebrate my thirteenth birthday. My mom shared my love of dance, and she wanted to show it. We arrived in the early evening. The lights were dimmed, and we were the only people in the club at that hour. My mom sat at a round booth in the corner, slowly nursing a cold Corona. She looked elegant in a fashionable light denim dress with a skirt that flared at the waist, and she wore classic nude heels over her nylon pantyhose. Her dirty-blonde hair was cut in a short bob with a few curls shaping her round face, and red lipstick perfectly accented her smile.

There was a large dance floor in the center of the room, and mirrors lined the back wall to highlight the adventures on it. It was the kind of place where local musicians would perform before they made it big, and it stood out in a Colorado mountain town that preferred country to disco. I took a sip of my Shirley Temple and bit into the extra cherry the bartender had added to my glass. My siblings and I sat together in the booth with our mom. Rose was dressed in her Disney princess nightgown, and Richard had brought his cowboy boots for a night on the town.

The music playing overhead shifted to a familiar tune as the slow intro to Madonna's "Like a Prayer" played in the background. I'd been practicing a dance to that song every night after school. The DJ made a welcoming wave toward me and pointed to the dance floor. I glanced at my mom, who was beaming with joy as her grand birthday surprise unfolded. She had talked with the nightclub owner and arranged for me to perform my solo choreography.

I made my way to the dance floor. Here was my opportunity to let loose, to be free for a few minutes. I was dressed head to toe in black. My outfit included a casual short-sleeved T-shirt tucked into a denim skirt trimmed in black lace. I also wore black tights that fit into my new ankle boots, which made me feel like Madonna herself. I felt more sophisticated than the thirteen years of life I was celebrating that evening. I appreciated my mom's wild effort to bring her newly minted teenager to the dance club, but as I took my place at center stage, leaving my Shirley Temple half-finished, I felt equal parts titillated and chagrined. I know my mom meant well, but some part of me felt weird dancing in a club at thirteen years old. Was I breaking the rules? I wasn't sure if kids were allowed on the dance floor, and I never wanted to break the rules.

I was a bit nervous yet also excited and ready to show off the signature choreography I'd been practicing and committing to memory over the last few months of rehearsing my *Star Search* moves in our living room. Though the club's wood floor felt sticky, it was still an upgrade from the shag carpet I had been practicing on at home.

The nightclub's outer edges darkened as the spotlights found me on the dance floor. I took my place kneeling on the floor with my head down as the music continued. I pulled my arms toward me as I leaned back, passionately lip-syncing to the lyrics. As Madonna sang her prayer, I felt desperation in my body. My passion for dance swept over me, and all I wanted was to express my heart along with the music. I didn't care if people were looking or what they thought. The opportunity to escape into my happy place and showcase my *Star Search* moves brought a deep glow into my body and opened up a playful side that I rarely got to experience in my day-to-day life.

A few couples joined the audience and made their way to the booths that lined the edges of the dance floor. I leveled up my performance, my skirt twirling with each spin. I started to feel the glow from the bright lights and my own passionate dancing as my body merged with the music's prayer. All the talent shows I'd danced in felt like they'd been preparation for this moment. When the song ended, I took a small bow and the scattering of people in the club at nine o'clock on a Wednesday night clapped for me. I stepped off the dance floor, sweating and breathing heavily, and thought, *That was fun.* Like your favorite roller coaster at an amusement park, dangerous and thrilling, I wanted to go again. My whole body was infused with joy.

Standing tall, and a little out of breath, I made my way back to my smiling family and my abandoned Shirley Temple. I took

Prologue

a sip of my drink and toasted to my mom, who had created this adventure for me—she beamed with pride at her daughter dancing the night away on a school night. My sister clapped obnoxiously, excited to see her big sister take a turn on the dance floor and happy to be up way past her bedtime. I took a deep swig of my virgin drink and basked in the afterglow.

Part I
A Rigid Ballet

A traditional dance that requires great discipline with structured and controlled movements. Women ballet dancers usually dance en pointe (on their toes), either alone or in partnership, and there is little room for creative expression.

1

For Better
or for Worse

"Will you marry me?" Morey whispered in my ear.

I looked down at the three sparkling diamonds glistening on a shiny platinum band. They were illuminated by a bright light hidden in the jewelry box, and the ring shone like an art piece.

Waves crashed in front of me like a lullaby, gently rolling in and out with each breath of the Pacific. A hazy cloud wrapped around the moon, dimming its light on an otherwise clear California night. Morey's arms wrapped around me like a freshly washed blanket warm from the dryer, and I took a deep breath. Did I want to marry Morey? I hadn't expected that question so soon, after only a few weeks of dating. I mean, who proposes so quickly? What would my parents think?

Things had moved quickly. Nora, my best friend and Morey's sister, had introduced us at their cousin's wedding on New Year's Day, and Morey had revealed himself as my secret admirer on Valentine's Day. I'd just started the spring semester of my freshman year at the University of Colorado Boulder and was intrigued by Morey's email promises of an adventurous life, especially after a childhood full of obligations to my siblings, but I hadn't expected this romance train to keep accelerating at such a rapid pace. I knew I didn't love him. I hadn't felt a spark when I came to Southern California to spend spring break with him and we kissed for the first time.

Dancing on My Own Two Feet

Morey's breath warmed my neck as he waited for me to answer. I knew in my gut that marriage was a terrible idea. Everything in my body and mind told me to run, but I didn't have the heart to say no to his proposal. As I lay there, I tried to convince myself to say no, which should have been easy. Would have been easy. But honoring myself, saying what I felt and needed, was a muscle I'd barely exercised in my life. It was especially difficult in the face of such conviction from Morey. My fear of making him feel bad, angry, or upset overwhelmed the care or concern I might have had for my own wishes and feelings. My mind flashed on the pain I'd felt when I saw the sadness in my parents' eyes as they parted ways. Back then, at age twelve, I'd wanted to make their suffering go away. I'd been conditioned since that day to try and keep the peace at all costs, regardless of whatever personal needs I might have to ignore in the process. I didn't want to feel the pain of rejecting Morey.

And I longed for the excitement of moving to a new place and not having anyone to take care of. I imagined starting anew and claiming my own life. After nearly a decade of helping to raise my three siblings (including watching my six-year-old sister on the weekends so my mom, now a single mother, could have some support), I was hungry for a break. My gap year after high school hadn't made up for the intensity of my teenage years, when I managed my family obligations while achieving academic success. I didn't want to be a pseudo-mom to my youngest siblings anymore. I just wanted to be me. I imagined myself as a young woman traveling the world and pursuing my passion for dance and European culture. I felt a little giddy at the prospect but also nervous. Besides, Morey's initial courtship emails had indicated his desire to travel the world and live an extraordinary life, too. So, despite a tiny, nearly inaudible inner voice that kept telling me to run the other way, I didn't. I couldn't listen to it.

The crisp air of that early spring night swirled around us, the brisk breeze willing me to answer Morey's question. Unorganized thoughts raced in my mind during the milliseconds that passed before the words found their way to my lips. California certainly wasn't Europe, but it wasn't Colorado either. I was ready for a change, and the thought of leaving my familial obligations behind me in one fell swoop was tempting.

"Yes," I heard myself reply as if from a great distance. I felt disembodied as I said it out loud. Morey's arms tightened around me, nearly suffocating me.

I gently disentangled myself, though I felt like prying his arms away. "Of course I will." I attempted a smile and put on the ring to show it to him, releasing myself from his hold.

Three sizes too big, it flopped around on my ring finger. I felt queasy as I moved it to my thumb for safekeeping. The dangling rock should have been an omen. I looked down at the sparkle on my left thumb. The diamonds were beautiful, but the setting felt more like an anniversary band than an engagement ring, and it wasn't my style. Of course it wasn't—we barely knew each other. I squeezed my fingers together to keep the ring from sliding off as we walked hand in hand to the car. We kept the conversation light, Morey visibly relieved that I had said yes. I hid the awkwardness I felt as we made our way to the airport and ignored the nausea welling up inside as I put on a good face for Morey, wanting to keep things positive. When I boarded my flight from California back to Colorado, I was a newly engaged woman. I tried not to throw up.

I looked out the window of our hotel room overlooking the Las Vegas Strip. The desert wind had calmed, but there were still remnants of a golden haze of sand floating across the horizon. The sun was starting to set, bouncing off the glass exteriors of the high-rises and creating an amber glow across the sky.

"Hello, my love," Morey said, coming behind to embrace me.

"Are you ready to become husband and wife?" We'd been engaged for two months. Morey kissed the small of my neck. As he drew near, the smell of his aftershave repulsed me, a reaction that was becoming too common.

I tried not to gag. My stomach was already tied in knots of anticipation. My intuition continued to scold me, and I knew in my heart that I didn't want to marry Morey. What if the friends and family members who'd raised concerns about being too young to marry were right? We barely knew each other, and my feelings didn't seem like those of a bride-to-be. I tried to tell myself these were mere nerves. I had planned to express my apprehension to Morey's sister a few days before, but I couldn't get the words out. She'd helped bring us together and was so excited that we were becoming sisters. I didn't want to let her down. My stomach tightened as I thought about hurting Morey if I walked away. *What kind of person would I be if I didn't follow through on a promise?* I couldn't back out now.

"Yes, my love," I sputtered, feeling numb. Luckily, feeling numb had its rewards, and I'd gotten used to it.

I didn't want to be in such a hurry to get married, but I'd spent my high school years in an ultra-conservative Christian youth group and vowed to save myself for my husband. I didn't want to live with a man before marriage, either. I'd spent years focusing on honoring God in my relationships, so much so that I'd penned an editorial in my high school newspaper about the perils of teen dating and had only recently been allowing myself to hold hands and kiss. Morey seemed enthusiastic to make things official. He was eager to plan the details of our secret elopement and used his credit card to pay for everything. It was hard to stop his excitement or the plans that were already in motion.

"Let's get ready," Morey suggested as he retreated to the bathroom to don his Hawaiian shirt and khaki slacks, jolting me out of my thoughts.

My stomach grumbled and my nerves accelerated as my blood sugar descended along with my mood. Our drive from Morey's home in California to Las Vegas had taken longer than expected, and we'd barely made it to the courthouse to get our marriage license before our limo arrived to take us to the chapel. There wasn't time to eat anything now.

I had chosen a light, flowy Hawaiian summer dress with hues of green and blue turquoise for the ceremony, but now it seemed rather silly. Morey thought a Hawaiian theme would make the event more festive. I watched him put on the wooden lei that he'd bought at Tommy Bahama. The colorful attire added to my impression of how surreal this was. I found myself craving a white wedding gown and all the old, new, borrowed, and blue trimmings; a veil and long train; mother of the bride and attendants. If only my dad were there to give me away and dance with me afterward. I'd always imagined my family celebrating such an important day with me, but Morey thought it would be special to keep it a secret. I was nervous to let my parents know we had eloped, especially since they had never met him. I had worried about maintaining a long-distance relationship while honoring my desire to save myself until marriage, which created a sense of urgency. Besides, money was always tight in my family, and I didn't want to burden my dad with the expense of a big wedding. I hoped my family would understand when I told them.

Morey hummed tunelessly in the background, excited and antsy to get going. I put on a strapless bra, cinching my chest tightly and snapping each hook into place. I stepped into my floral halter top dress and added a few leis of fake pink and yellow flowers as I laced up a pair of three-inch white platform heels, the day's only traditional element. I pulled half of my short, wavy brown locks into a clip and added some red lipstick to complete my look. I stared at my face in the mirror on the back of the bathroom door and tried to exhale the butterflies that floated inside of me.

I returned to the window, took a deep breath, and saw the extra-long white limousine waiting in the roundabout in front of our hotel, ready to take us to the chapel. I felt like I was waltzing through a dream.

Morey grabbed my hand, squeezing it hard, and I gave him a gentle smile.

"Let's go," he said as I followed him out the door.

"Hi. Are you Morey?" the driver asked after we made our way into the warm spring evening.

"Yes, I am. And this is Jennifer, my budding bride." Morey beamed with pride as he wrapped his arm around me.

This would be my first time in a limo, and I felt more like I was going to prom than getting ready to promise my life to someone I barely knew. We made our way to the back seat, watching as the driver secured the glass plate to offer privacy. There was sparkling nonalcoholic cider in a little fridge next to the door, but I wasn't interested in drinking or in privacy. I laughed when I realized that I was twenty and about to commit to one of the most serious and binding adult contracts one could make, yet the state of Nevada still considered me too young to enjoy an alcoholic drink. The limo accelerated smoothly as we moved along the strip. We opened the sunroof and I tried to imagine I was a celebrity getting a private tour of the city, waving to my fans— any fantasy to avoid the uncomfortable reality a little bit longer. After a ten-minute drive, the limo slowed as we pulled up to the entrance of the Little White Chapel.

The name adequately described the venue's charm. There was a small steeple with an open chapel in the distance, and a narrow walkway lined with man-made waterfalls created a pathway to the altar. A few Internet searches had drawn us to this location, which looked like a venue from the movies. Morey and I took our time getting out of the limo and giving our driver another handshake before he waited for us to take care of business.

Morey grabbed my hand and escorted me along the path to the altar. I took a moment to notice his features as we headed to the check-in desk. He had an uncanny resemblance to Ben Affleck with perfectly styled dark hair and glossy, chiseled cheeks that compressed when he smiled. At nearly six feet tall, his height barely exceeded mine with my platform heels, and his Hawaiian shirt hung loosely from his slim frame. I longed to see him in a black tux, like the one he'd worn for his cousin's wedding nearly five months earlier, when we'd found ourselves drawn to each other on the dance floor for the first time. I had felt the heat of chemistry that evening as we lost ourselves to the beat of the music. Yet, in this moment, even his good looks couldn't make up for the lack of attraction I felt for him.

"Hello," Morey said enthusiastically to the receptionist, who would serve as our witness. "We're here to get married."

"Yes, of course. Come with me."

She brought us to the front of a small room where pink silk carnations made an arch over the altar. An elderly gentleman in a white suit approached us.

"Hello," he said. "I will be your minister performing the ceremony. Welcome." Then he turned to me and asked, "Who's giving you away?"

I shook my head, indicating that Morey and I would be the only people participating in the ceremony. He motioned us to the altar. Morey and I faced each other, holding hands. His palms were sweating.

"Jennifer, do you take Morey to be your lawfully wedded husband? To love and to cherish, in sickness and in health, for as long as you both shall live?" The minister went straight to the vows. There was no time for foreplay in this event.

"Uh, I . . . do." I couldn't stop the giggles bubbling up inside me.

The officiant glared at me as if to say, *This is for real, young lady. Are you sure you know what you're doing?*

I was nervous and hyperaware of how fake everything seemed as I stood surrounded by artificial flowers and a pasteboard chapel, pronouncing my love to a man I didn't feel fond of. It was like a nightmare I couldn't wake up from. Getting married without any of our friends or family present—not even Morey's sister, who'd been my best friend for years—felt surreal.

The officiant repeated the vows to Morey, who eagerly said "I do" without hesitation.

"Congratulations! You may kiss the bride."

With that, Morey leaned in for a wet, sloppy kiss. I feared I might throw up as I pushed down the sick, crawling feeling in the pit of my stomach. *What have I done?*

Barely ten minutes after we arrived, the receptionist signed our paperwork and we were officially husband and wife. We took a few photos by the man-made river flowing near the entrance, and I tried to force a smile. I'd just made the biggest mistake of my life. On the ride to the hotel, we toasted with some sparkling apple cider.

"Wifey, let's order room service and enjoy our first night as a married couple," Morey suggested when we made it back to our room, already unbuttoning his shirt.

I was beyond nervous about consummating our marriage. This would be my first time being intimate with a man. That we would begin the evening with dinner only made it worse. I was starving yet unexcited to eat. When the food arrived, the overpowering aroma of raw onions accompanying our burgers and fries sucked out of my bones any romantic desire I might have managed to generate. I retreated to the bath while Morey finished his dinner, trying to calm my nerves. I closed my eyes, sinking into the oversized jetted tub and losing myself in the aroma of the lavender bubble bath.

But I was soon jolted by reality when Morey slid in next to me. He began kissing me, and I tried to ignore the continued lack of chemistry between us. I wanted to prolong the foreplay for as long as possible, hoping it would get me in the mood or allow me a reprieve to try again tomorrow. But Morey didn't know slow.

"Honey, if we don't consummate our marriage, it won't be official," he said when he sensed my apprehension.

I wasn't sure why he was so concerned about making it official on our first night. Surely, many newlyweds are too tired on their wedding night and choose to be intimate at a later time. But I didn't know what I was doing and wasn't used to setting my own boundaries or asking for what I wanted or needed. My Christian upbringing hadn't prepared me for the delicacy of this moment. Spending so much time at church meant I'd missed the sex ed or schoolyard wisdom I would have met in a less conservative setting.

Morey helped me out of the bath, and I dried off and donned a white robe. He guided me toward the bed, and I could see he was ready for me. I had hoped his manly shape would appeal to my being, but there was still no spark. Morey didn't pick up on my subtle cues of nervousness as I took a few minutes to join him, unable to even fake a smile. My procrastination attempts were futile, so I retreated into his arms and let him take over. He was experienced and had lived more in his twenty-two years than I had lived in my twenty. Morey knew what to do and I went along with it, holding back the tears as pain made its way through my body. I craved someone who would be patient with me and wait for me to be ready, married or not. I felt his weight on me, and the uncomfortable pressure of body parts. I wasn't sure what to do with myself, but he was eventually satisfied that we were "officially" husband and wife. I rolled over and tried to sleep while he effortlessly dozed off next to me, clearly unaware of my discomfort. I was sure things would get better once I got the hang of it.

In the early morning hours, I couldn't stop staring at the neon alarm clock next to the bedside table and turned my back to Morey as tears rolled down my cheeks. I tried to fall asleep, but instead, I felt the heat of regret growing in my core.

The tears continued to fall in the morning, and I did my best to hide them from Morey. He was not my person. I wondered, *How can I take it back? Should I get an annulment before we leave Vegas?* I didn't know what to do. With little time to think, we loaded our things into Morey's Mazda and made the four-hour drive back to his home in Southern California. The car ride was silent, and Morey eventually admitted he did not want children. I had always dreamed of a big family. *How could this be my life? Surely, this was grounds for an annulment.* Tears rolled down my cheeks as I took it all in. I kept my gaze outside the passenger window, watching the desert sand stretch across the horizon, continuing to hide my emotions. Something inside me wanted this to succeed, couldn't admit things were wrong, needed to be a good girl. That feeling was too strong to let me walk away.

The next morning, I returned to my dorm in Colorado to finish the spring semester of my freshman year of college.

I printed the wedding photos at the local grocery store in my hometown a few weeks after the wedding. I was flipping through them in the parking lot when my dad approached me, getting ready to start his shift as the seafood manager.

"What do you have there?" he asked inquisitively, reminding me of Curious George.

"Oh, nothing," I replied, frantically stuffing the envelope of pictures into my purse. I gave my dad a quick hug and wished him well as I made the journey back to my car.

My mom was the only person I'd told about the wedding, and thankfully, she'd offered her blessing. She even sold her bike to give us a $100 wedding gift. Mothers are like that—they really do love you unconditionally, even when you make what will turn out to be a monumental mistake. I wondered if she had compassion for me since she knew what it was like to get married so young and wanted to do what she could to help set us up for success.

That evening, I knew I had to come clean. I was sitting at the kitchen table getting ready to have dinner with my dad and stepmom when I blurted it out.

"I got married a few weeks ago in Vegas." Silence filled the room.

"You did *what*?"

My stepmom froze, her hands filled with a bowl of pasta she nearly dropped on the floor. As she slowly came to life, tears rolled down her cheeks and she sat next to me, burying her head in her hands. "What have you done?" was all she could muster.

I pleaded my case to my father, feeling like I was still a little girl trying to avoid being in trouble. "Morey and I eloped in Las Vegas. We wanted to tell you, but we thought it would be fun to do something special, just the two of us. Besides, I know money is tight, and it was an inexpensive way to make things official. We're hoping to have a reception next year to celebrate with the family. I didn't feel comfortable moving in with Morey without being married. I know it's a shock and I feel so uncomfortable sharing this with you after it's done, but I'd really love to have your blessing."

My father looked shocked. "How will you continue your studies if you're married? You have such a bright future ahead of you, and this will make it harder to stay on track."

The pit in my stomach grew even bigger. My heart ached as I tried to explain my decision to get married at twenty to a man my family had never met after three months of long-distance dating. My explanations rang hollow even to me. I tried to understand my own reasons and came up short.

It was the first time that I'd visibly disappointed my father. It was also the first impulsive decision I'd ever made. It was already done, so it was time to make the best of it.

Dancing on My Own Two Feet

～❦〜

One month later, the blue sky was blinding and the sun shone down on me while I finished packing up my dorm and prepared to say goodbye to family and friends so I could join Morey and start our life together in California. He waited for me at my mom's house while I finished gathering my things. I looked down at a Winnie the Pooh box filled with my childhood treasures: handwritten programs highlighting my neighborhood talent shows, an acceptance letter to a preprofessional ballet company when I was fifteen (a grand feat after only starting professional training at age fourteen), and my pointe shoes, frazzled from overuse.

A few tears fell as I acknowledged how much I'd needed the solace of the dance studio during my teenage years and how much relief it had provided during the fifteen hours I spent there each week, free from my obligations at home. It was truly a sacred space. I remembered how excited I'd felt when I was admitted to the dance company as a principal dancer. Even though the yards of sequins and tulle weren't cheap, my dance instructor was willing to work with me by offering me a scholarship and part-time teaching opportunities to offset tuition costs. I'd been thankful there was a way to make it work, though I couldn't help but compare myself to the other students, who had received formal training since they were toddlers and whose parents seemed to cover the costs with ease. I felt shame mixed with pride at my self-sufficiency. But no matter how tenuous the financial situation was, I felt beautiful and free once I was in the studio.

As I packed a few pairs of old tights, leotards, and skirts into the box, I felt as if I had been transported back to the dance studio. I remembered the way my body had relaxed into a delightful, magical world each time I opened a brand-new pair of pink Bloch ballet tights and wrapped a chiffon skirt around my waist. I felt that I was where I belonged as the crisp smell of new tights mixed with a few buds of sweat. Even though my toes were blistered from the plaster box of my pointe shoes, I felt intensely alive and happy when I was dancing. As soon as the music started and I touched my hand to the barre, then executed that first tendu and the initial plié in first position, I relinquished all my worries and cares. There at the ballet studio, I didn't have to think about money, my siblings, or my parents; it all fell away the minute I extended my arms, pointed my toes, and relished expressing myself.

Now, as I placed my pointe shoes and dance letters back into the box, I found a picture from my thirteenth birthday and my debut dance performance at Springers, my mom smiling from ear to ear. I hugged the picture, remembering the magic of performing that night, my sassy smile and attitude on full display in the photo. As I continued to search through the box, a few childhood poems emerged in my precious cursive handwriting, through which I expressed the multitude of emotions that I processed during my early years. Some of them were admittedly dark for a young woman, but I stopped for a few minutes when I came across one that I wrote when Chelsea, my littlest sister, was born after my mom started another relationship. I was fourteen then, and my parents had been divorced for two years.

> *It was a warm spring morning, as peaceful to be*
> *When my little sister was brought to me*
> *With big bright blue eyes, and her bald little head*
> *She looked like a flower in her little bed*
> *I promised to love her and teach her what's right*
> *Because of the feeling of that precious sight*

My heart warmed as I dug deeper into the treasure chest. At the bottom of the box were mounds of awards, medals, and honors highlighting my academic success, including the announcement that I was salutatorian. I remembered staring up each night at the awards I'd hung on my bedroom wall, shoring up my sense of accomplishment against the obligation I often felt at home, always trying to make my parents proud. I was never satisfied unless I had a string of perfect As on my report cards. I had just received my first and only B during my spring semester of college, something I chalked up to being distracted by Morey's courtship.

I recognized that despite the challenges I'd navigated after my parents split up, I'd made something of myself and pursued my passions, undeterred by the bumpy road along the way. As I continued packing my things, I placed brochures from colleges across the world in my treasure chest, reminding myself that one day, I would make my dream of traveling the world come true. I paused for a few minutes when I found a picture of my church youth group surrounded by a group of young children in Mexico. My heart leapt with joy at the thought of starting my own family one day, but then I remembered Morey didn't want children. When my phone rang, I swallowed the emotions that were bubbling up inside.

"You ready?" Morey asked, jolting me out of my nostalgia. "Your family and I are ready to say goodbye."

"Yes. I'll be leaving shortly." I closed my treasure box and turned off the light, wiping the tears from the corner of my eyes.

When I arrived back at my mom's house, I could see my mom, dad, brother, and sisters in front of the house ready to say goodbye.

I loaded the last of my things into Morey's car and hugged my family. I was relieved that I was getting a positive send-off before we made the cross-country drive to start our married life together. They'd only met Morey a few days earlier, and we all were putting on our best smiles, trying to get along.

"I love you guys and I'll visit soon. Don't worry," I said, trying to stay calm.

Each person embraced me with tears in their eyes. Morey's sister, Nora, and two of my childhood best friends, twin sisters Zoey and Quinn, joined the group and hugged me with deep conviction. Holding back my tears, I got in the car and waved from the passenger seat. As the car lurched forward, I kept my gaze in front of me, not brave enough to look back.

2

California Dreaming

Morey and I arrived in California after several days of driving across the Western plains and desert. The hot summer day dissolved into a cool mist that refreshed my senses as the sun set in the distance. I took a deep breath and felt the fresh California air welcome me to my new home, a condo complex in Orange County halfway between LA and San Diego. We parked Morey's car in a detached garage and walked through a series of spiraling paths to an older condo complex with beige stucco exteriors and small garden porches. It had an eerie effect that was common in California: providing an urban oasis even though the complex was next to a major freeway. We could always hear traffic swooshing along nearby. Watching palm trees glimmer in the sparkling streetlights made me feel at ease, and the street noise somehow relaxed me.

"Here we are." Morey welcomed me with a flourish as we approached the condo we rented from his father. He opened the door and awkwardly carried me over the threshold.

When he put me down, I looked around and refreshed my memory. There was a dark blue sofa bed along a mirrored wall, a makeshift kitchen table in the back nook, a few electric guitars and an amplifier in the corner, and several floor lamps that only dimly lit the small living space. I made my way to the bedroom and quietly placed my things in a corner, taking a deep breath. For better or worse, this was home.

"We made it," I mustered, forcing a smile as Morey handed me a drink and I made my way to the living room. I settled into the sofa to take in my new surroundings.

I took a gulp of my (still virgin) drink. I wasn't sure what my life would look like, but I told myself I would do my best to be a good wife and finish college. I shushed the voice inside that screamed at feeling so unsettled. Instead, I committed myself to establishing a new routine—I'd go to school, go to the beach, and enjoy time with Morey as we figured out our new life together. Maybe I would even dance a little to bring joy back to my body, though I already felt that part of myself, which had once meant so much, dissolving away before this freshly minted newlywed self.

This was the first time I'd lived so far from home. I was already anticipating the homesickness that would follow in the days ahead. I knew I'd miss my family. I'd miss taking my six-year-old sister, Chelsea, to the park and doing laundry at my mom's while she made me lunch. I'd miss the grand mountains that took my breath away each day when I awoke in my dorm room. I'd even miss the moments with my brother Richard and sister Rose, now eighteen and fifteen, that we'd endured as we figured out how to raise ourselves after our parents' divorce. I'd miss my old dance studio and being a choreographer for the church youth group. I had traveled several thousand miles to live in a place where I didn't know anyone, including my husband. But that had been the plan. I had to make it work to prove I hadn't made a mistake.

After a few weeks in California, I was longing to stretch my dance moves and share an intimate moment with my husband. Part of my initial attraction to Morey had been his ability to break loose on the dance floor at his cousin's wedding. I'd dreamed of finding a dance partner in life, and despite our bumpy start, I was hopeful that dance could be our silver lining. One night, a month after moving into the condo and beginning our married life together, we visited a nightclub. I looked down at the dance floor, salivating as I watched the young professionals getting their groove on. It made me yearn for my own sensual encounter with Morey.

"Morey, let's dance. Let's see those breakdancing moves again," I flirted, pulling him toward me.

"Nah, that's lame," he replied, and pulled away.

"What do you mean, it's lame? We had so much fun dancing at your cousin's wedding last year—I thought that was when you realized there were sparks between us. You know I love to dance. I thought we would be a dancing couple in life." I couldn't understand why he was acting like that.

"I don't want to dance again. It's silly to be flaunting ourselves on the dance floor. Let's stay up here and have a drink." I was in shock as he turned his head and continued to toss back his bottle of Bud Light.

I kept my gaze on the dance floor. *Wait. I married this guy on the basis of dancing with him—at least we'd have that!—and he's not interested?* I felt like I'd been punched in the gut, as if the air inside me had been pushed out. Deep regret filled my core, and I wasn't sure how to react. A few minutes later, Morey summoned me out of the club.

On the ride home, I tried to reconcile what had just happened with the image I'd had of our future. Sure, we hadn't danced much after becoming husband and wife, even in our living room, but I hadn't thought much of it. Now, faced with a vehement *no*, I wondered if my desire for Morey to be my dancing partner for life had been a fantasy that was crashing down. But I found myself nervous to bring it up. I was trying to attune to his wishes instead of listening to and expressing my own. That was how I'd responded during childhood whenever I felt tension in my house. Yet I couldn't imagine a life without dance.

Four weeks later, after I finished a ballet class at a local studio, I had another strange encounter with Morey.

"Hey, tomato face," he teased when I returned home. "It seems like you're overheated. Are you sure it's a good idea to be dancing at your age? Maybe it's best left for your childhood."

"Uh, I don't know. I'm just out of practice. I need to get back into it," I offered, but I was embarrassed, which only added to the redness in my cheeks.

Instead of pushing back, I retreated. I was afraid of engaging in conflict, and I wasn't used to defending my own needs. I'd been a sensitive child, and I'd hidden in my room whenever my dad raised his voice. I'd crank my music to avoid the tumultuous fighting sounds that ended my parents' marriage. *Maybe I could give up my dance classes for a while. I don't want another confrontation with Morey.* So, at the ripe old age of twenty, I hung up my dance shoes.

While I never fell in love with Morey, we got into an easy rhythm during that first year of marriage. I slowly became more comfortable in my new surroundings, and, for the most part, Morey and I got along. We spent every evening together, making dinner and cuddling on the couch watching movies. Each of us gained fifteen pounds from inactivity.

On my twenty-first birthday, I celebrated the milestone in my kitchen by blowing out a candle on a chocolate cupcake while dressed in Winnie the Pooh pajamas my mom had mailed to me the week before. Morey and I played guitar together with the front door of our apartment open, serenaded by a cool California breeze. Our little spitfire Chihuahua, Maggie, barked as if to sing along. I told myself dogs were a good enough substitute for children as I tried to embrace the idea of living kid-free. Now of legal drinking age, I toasted with my first official shot of whiskey and enjoyed a simple evening at home. Despite whatever misgivings I may have had about Morey, I believed we could be happy. Our intimacy had gained momentum, and he was mostly kind and caring toward me. I was starting to appreciate his easygoing nature and the kind of spontaneity that could lead us to embrace each other so quickly.

I'd never intended to abandon my studies when I moved, so I quickly enrolled at the local community college. Money was tight, and that was a cost-effective way to work toward my degree while waiting to gain California residency and enroll at a state school. Morey encouraged me to continue, and during my first semester back at school, I pivoted from studying molecular biology and French to an accounting major. I planned to take the CPA exams after I got my bachelor's degree. Morey took classes with me, and we listened to his favorite heavy metal music in the car on the way to our political science class each morning, enjoying the day-to-day life of two young students working to make ends meet. A year into our marriage, we moved out of the condo and began renting a two-bedroom house in Long Beach. We spent our weekends test-driving cars and eating free hot dogs at the dealership, a cheap form of entertainment. Life seemed to be a freewheeling romp, and even our attempts to make ends meet felt like an adventure—the kind you imagine young married people go through on their way to the white picket-fenced, two-car American dream.

When my college graduation finally came, my parents, siblings, grandpa, and cousins traveled to California to celebrate. We played cards and splashed in the pool at the Embassy Suites, where we had a graduation luncheon with Morey and his family. It was the first time both families were together. This gathering stood in for the wedding reception we never had. It felt wonderful to have everyone together, and a kind of peace washed over me when I realized I had achieved my childhood dream of earning a college degree, the first in my immediate family. I also had a job offer from a large public accounting firm. I was starting to feel like I had made it.

But Morey lost his job early in our marriage and struggled to find another one. With Morey out of work, it seemed like I might need to be the breadwinner, which I told myself was okay—I was no stranger to supporting others. Although I would never admit it to anyone else, deep down, I liked the addictive rush of endorphins from feeling needed.

While things seemed okay on the surface, I often found myself at odds with Morey. One weekend, we decided to get away and drove down the coast to visit his cousin and her boyfriend. We stayed up late hanging by the pool. Her boyfriend was a talker, and he went on and on and on all night. Though I was tired from the drive, my good-girl upbringing kicked in, so I kept nodding patiently as he continued his droning monologue.

On the ride home the next day, Morey screamed at me. "Are you trying to flirt with my cousin's boyfriend? Why were you listening to him so attentively for over an hour? Are you cheating on me?"

"I was just trying to be polite," I sputtered, shocked at his reaction.

"Well, don't do it again. This was embarrassing." He spat his words at me, still angry.

"I'm sorry if you thought I was flirting." I appeased him, confused about why it was such a big deal.

I was raised to listen when others spoke. At some level, I realized I felt threatened by Morey, and I wasn't sure why.

3

Too Hot
to Handle

I t was the middle of August, one year into my new job, when
Morey and I were driving home from Phoenix. He still didn't
have a job and had joined me on a work trip. We felt like roy-
alty charging room service at a fancy hotel room to my expense
account. We started to dream out loud about buying our own
house, white picket fence and all. During our getaway, we looked
at some properties in Arizona. But we had second thoughts after
seeing tires being burned in the scorching 110-degree heat along
the freeway. The cool breeze from the car's air-conditioning was
refreshing, although with such intense heat outside, it quickly
dissipated and felt stale.

Without warning, about two hours outside of Phoenix, Morey
pulled over. Was there something wrong with the car?

"I can't breathe," he cried, gasping for air. "I feel like I am having a heart attack." He clutched his throat. "What should I do?"

I wanted to panic. I was twenty-five years old and wasn't
equipped to provide medical care, having forgotten all the
CPR training I'd had as a teenage babysitter. But somehow, my
instincts took over.

"Move over. Let's get you to an ER," I said forcefully as Morey
pulled himself over the car's center panel and into the passenger
seat.

I drove as Morey took deep breaths, trying to calm down.

"Are you okay? Can you hang on a few more minutes?" I kept asking. I alternated between looking at the road and looking at Morey.

"Yes, but hurry," he replied, a terrified look in his eyes.

Ten minutes later, I pulled up to the entrance of the closest hospital. Morey had calmed down and his breathing had stabilized, but he was still shaken. I helped him out of the car and into the ER.

"Please help," I yelled as I entered the lobby. "My husband thinks he's having a heart attack and can't breathe!"

I helped a nurse put Morey in a wheelchair, and she transported him to a place beyond two large electronic doors to be evaluated.

I waited in the lobby for several hours. When Morey came out, he looked defeated.

"Everything was normal. They ran an EKG and blood tests and nothing serious came back. The doctors think it was an anxiety or panic attack, possibly provoked by thinking about moving to the desert. I'm not so sure. But let's go home." Morey was already on his way out the door and walking back to our car.

"Okay," I replied, not quite sure what to do or think.

We drove the remaining two hours in silence.

When we got home, we took a shower and crawled into bed. As I fell asleep, I hoped this scare was just that.

Unfortunately, the events of that evening replayed week after week for months. After that ER visit, Morey and I visited every specialist we could find, but they sent us home each time. No one could give us a proper diagnosis. With each doctor's visit, Morey's energy became more depleted and he lost more hope.

"I can't do it anymore. It's too much," he said after a year's worth of doctor visits and diagnostic tests. He decided never to go back to the doctor's office again.

Dancing on My Own Two Feet

～❧

As I began my second year at my job in public accounting, I wasn't sure what to do. Morey's episodes were a near-daily occurrence, and I was struggling to manage both work and home. Suddenly, I was a full-time caregiver again. That skill had gone a bit rusty since I stopped caring for my siblings, but I soon discovered caregiving was deep in my muscle memory and nearly second nature to me. I quickly pivoted to making meals and managing all the household activities while also trying to hold down a relatively new job.

I'd gotten some positive feedback during my first year at the firm, but working full-time in the office while being a caregiver at home grew increasingly difficult. Every day, I felt nervousness in the pit of my stomach and my heart felt crushed. I was convinced I had to quit my job to take care of Morey full-time. I started contacting recruiters to see if I could find a job that was willing to let me work from home. It was the only possible solution I could think of. The first recruiter I talked to presented me with another option, suggesting that I reach out to my supervisors and ask for support instead.

Talk to my supervisors to see if they can work with me? I hadn't even considered that possibility. My masterful problem-solving skills had left me shortsighted. I paused for a minute, grateful for a new avenue to explore.

It was the early 2000s, and I didn't know of anyone in my company who had a formal telework arrangement, especially at the staff associate level. But I knew the company offered other flexible work arrangements, some of which the partners on my team had utilized. I hoped my team would be willing to work with me once I pleaded my case.

"How can I help you?" my supervisor, Mandy, asked after we settled in during my next office visit. Her eyes were kind and her spirit was gentle even though she was a towering accounting goddess at six feet tall. I was thankful to have found a mentor like her so early in my career.

Taking a breath, I launched in. "Well, I know I've mentioned that my husband has been sick. It's starting to get severe, and I think I need to be home with him during the day to care for him. I know that it's not common to telework as a staff member, but I don't want to leave the company. I wanted to see if we might be able to make something work."

I briskly rattled off all the details of the possible arrangement, indicating how I'd thought it through, showing my work, neatly ticking off all the boxes I thought my boss might want to hear about commute, security, and so forth. I smiled brightly and reassuringly, willing her to say yes, the organized and responsible side I'd relied on in my youth emerging from dormancy. In that moment, I realized how desperate I was. It might not be easy to find another firm willing to work in such an unorthodox way, and I needed a job.

"Jennifer, of course we can try. I know things haven't been easy. You have tremendous potential. It sounds like you have thoughtfully considered how we can make this work. Let's give it a try, and if it doesn't work out, I'll help you find another job after busy season." She smiled reassuringly.

Relieved, I slumped in my chair. Mandy had given me a lifeline and I was grasping it with all I had.

Teleworking as a staff associate for three months during busy season was a grand experiment, and my job was on the line. I became an expert at taking care of Morey while solving accounting problems in my head at home. I worked all hours of the day to make sure my tasks were completed on time and Morey was cared for. The pointe dancer in me reemerged, balancing responsibilities like a delicate relevé, trying to keep everything in the air while I pirouetted from one precarious task to the next.

In the early days of working from home, Morey thanked me when I gave acupressure massages to control his anxiety attacks, and his eyes seemed grateful when I made accommodations to limit external stimuli and help manage his symptoms. But his illness, whatever it was, got worse to the point where he became housebound. I tried my best to pretend none of this mattered to me, that I wasn't disappointed to be a caregiver *again*, and that I didn't mind spending my twenties reading medical blogs instead of dancing in a club or going out with my husband on date night. I was used to adapting and making the most of things. *School, work, family obligations* had been my operating model since I was twelve, so unfortunately, it was an old familiar waltz. I thought, *Of course I'll figure out a way to do both caregiving and work.* I didn't see any other viable choice. I couldn't conceive of outsourcing his care or asking for help from friends or neighbors. *How could a good wife even consider such a thing?* Besides, he wasn't willing to accept help from anyone except me. He told me I was his safety person, and I believed it.

My childhood had demanded that I balance the different weights of my life, and my muscle memory was strong. I knew the steps to this dance better than even the *Star Search* number I'd danced by heart when I was thirteen. But it still hurt when I pulled a metaphorical hamstring trying to finish all my tasks.

Just as I thought I had this under my feet, my childhood best friends, Zoey and Quinn, moved from Colorado to Los Angeles. I longed to get together with them and have a makeshift social life. I finally decided that I could add "friend" to my dance card, and I made plans for a brunch with my besties in Hollywood to celebrate the end of busy season. I was afraid to tell Morey, so I left while he was asleep, hoping he wouldn't need me while I was gone.

It was foggy on the morning when we got together. The road north on the 405 looked like a scene out of Sleepy Hollow, and I struggled to see the Hollywood Sign perched in the distance when I parked my car behind the coffee shop where we'd made plans to meet. I was wearing a hot-pink blouse and had taken time to blow-dry my bobbed hair to feel more sophisticated for brunch with my ladies. The coffee shop was cozy, and ivy climbed the entrance to the patio where my friends were already seated, drinking skim lattes in large white porcelain mugs. I ran to embrace them.

"It's so great to see you both," I exclaimed, feeling just a tiny bit human being out in the company of adults and not dressed in pajamas.

"Jenn!" they shouted in unison. As twins, they were used to doing things together, and I'd always loved the energy and enthusiasm they brought to my life.

"My, how I've missed you! You can't even imagine. Tell me, how do you like LA so far? How are you adjusting? Wait, is that Marc Anthony sitting in the corner over there?" There was too much to catch up on, and my senses were in overdrive from getting out of my house and into the real world—or at least Hollywood—even for a moment.

"We miss you, too. LA is good, work is fun, and yes, that's Marc Anthony."

My friends took turns answering. We all laughed, and I joined them in enjoying a warm latte on the gloomy day.

Just as we were getting ready to order, my phone rang.

"One second, guys. It's Morey. Let me see if everything is okay."

My friends were still looking at the menu, their thoughts focused on what they wanted for brunch, oblivious to the bubbling nervousness I felt welling up beneath the surface.

"Hi, Morey. Is everything all right?" I hoped he was fine so I could enjoy this one day out.

"No, I'm not feeling well. I'm having anxiety and my chest hurts. Where are you? It's the weekend. I thought you would be home." He sounded annoyed and was clearly surprised I wasn't there with him.

"Oh, no. I'm sorry you aren't feeling well. I forgot to mention I was having brunch with the girls. We're in Hollywood. I can make it home soon, but we're just getting ready to order." I didn't want to go home yet.

"Can you come home *now*? I really need you." His tone told me he wouldn't take no for an answer.

I felt like two people were pulling me in different directions, stretching me physically thin, and I would tear in half if I didn't move one way or the other. I wanted to enjoy a few hours with my friends, but I couldn't figure out how to say no to Morey. Surely, he would be okay on his own for a few hours. But the pit opened in my stomach as I tried to imagine it. *How can I choose? Why do I have to?* I tried to hold back the tears blossoming in my eyes.

The waiter asked, "Did you ladies decide what you would like to order?" My friends nodded in unison.

As he turned to me, I muttered, "I'll take the eggs Benedict."

I put my phone in my purse. *It's only a couple of hours. I'll be home soon and take care of Morey. I don't have to choose between my friends and taking care of him. I can have both.*

I did my best to continue the conversation. Zoey and Quinn had both started new jobs, were decorating their new apartment in West Hollywood, and were bubbling over with all the bright enthusiasm you would expect from young women in their twenties who had just taken their first jobs in LA. They talked about the restaurants and clubs they were exploring and the men they were interested in or getting over.

I, on the other hand, felt like a jumbled ball of yarn. The knots in my stomach grew as I ate my eggs Benedict at super speed, barely listening to the twins and unable to contribute much to the conversation through the fog and the weight I carried. I needed to get home. Before my friends finished their last bites, we posted a quick selfie and I said goodbye.

"Ladies, I know this was a quick visit, but Morey needs me. I need to get home now. Let's try and do this again soon. Love you." I waved as I bolted to my car.

Once I was on the freeway, I drove as fast as I could. I was thankful that LA traffic had been kind to me that morning, allowing me to make it home in record time.

"Where have you been?" Morey nearly screamed when I finally entered through our front door. "I've been waiting for you for hours. This is serious. Don't do that again. I need you here." He was clearly aghast that I hadn't come home immediately after his call.

"Uh, sorry. Okay. I tried my best to come as quickly as I could, but I wanted to at least have a few minutes with my friends since I haven't seen them in years." I tried to explain, but my words faltered. It was no use.

"You should have known I would need you," was all Morey said as he turned to watch TV, calm now that I had arrived home.

A swirl of thoughts raced through my mind. *What just happened? Did I really need to rush home so quickly? Why does he seem fine now that I'm home?* I felt defeated, like I'd been tricked since Morey didn't seem to need me after all. Despite feeling that something was off, something that desperately needed to be aired between us, I couldn't bring myself to raise the subject. I thought about how unreasonable it was for him to expect that I would be home twenty-four seven, and I wanted to call him out on his unresponsiveness.

Something had shifted since our trip to Arizona, something that went beyond his obvious illness. I was deep into the caregiving swirl, and he desperately needed me, so I tried not to think about it too much. All I could see was that I had a hard time saying no when I was needed. I felt tethered by a string of guilt to meet his needs, and the string tightened each time I challenged his demands.

I made less effort after that day to connect with my friends in person. I slowly learned to live as a single married person. When I did go out, which wasn't often, I ended up eating alone at restaurants, envious of all the couples I saw enjoying meals together. I would take my meal in silence, and quickly, waiting for my phone's inevitable ring.

My busy-season attempt at teleworking had been such a success that my company allowed me to formally continue it. I was relieved that I didn't need to find another job, and I continued to be optimistic and creative when things at work and home became challenging. But I was always off-balance. Morey insisted that I not leave the house except to shop, and I learned to live in constant "plan B" mode. On one occasion, I'd planned to go to my client's office for an important meeting, but at the last minute, Morey begged me to stay home since he couldn't handle me being away.

"Would it be okay if I call in to the meeting instead?" I would ask my supervisor, feeling vulnerable and nervous with each new request that I added to my repertoire of flexible work arrangements.

"Of course," was Mandy's typical reply, but deep down, I wondered if she was getting tired of the constant litany of new accommodations.

Although things were generally going well at work, and I was even promoted to supervisor with Mandy's help (she "homeschooled" me on all the in-person training so I wouldn't miss out), they were deteriorating at home. Morey began sleeping during the day, which helped accommodate my work. But that meant I pulled a night shift to feed him dinner, waking at three in the morning since his illness, still undiagnosed, had nearly disabled him. The interrupted sleep stopped bothering me over time, and I learned to adjust. Having two bedrooms helped; we each had our own room to manage the different schedules. However, his emotional volatility got worse, which stretched my already-thin nerves. Morey continued getting upset if I wasn't home, and he even started blaming me for his illness.

"You aren't doing enough to help me figure out what's wrong with me." Morey huffed around the house, glaring at me after a bad allergy attack that happened when I tried to do a load of laundry while he was awake. I wanted to speak up, defend myself, and say I was doing what I could, but my body froze. My heart sank each time he said something like this. My vocal cords were paralyzed, and I didn't have the courage to respond. My body and spirit felt more and more compressed with each complaint that I internalized in silence. I began to grow apathetic and numb, and I just wanted peace.

"I told you not to take a shower during the day. I can't breathe from the steam when you open the bathroom door," he would call after me as I hurried to my room to get ready for work, another error added to my eternal tally.

I did my best to accommodate all the challenges. Between my responsibilities at work and at home, I would go to the Laundromat to prevent allergic reactions, and I only showered when he was asleep. I turned our storage room into a makeshift kitchen to avoid using the stovetop. Sometimes I felt inspired to find a creative solution, and yet the tasks and hardships were never-ending. I was solely responsible for managing the house, Morey's care, and the finances, and I had little time for myself. With Morey unable to leave the house, he spent most of the day in front of the

TV to keep his mind occupied. His family, who lived down the street, rarely visited, and I felt like I lived on a deserted island. I wondered, *How long can I continue like this?*

"You only seem to care about your work. What about *me*? Do you even love me?" That became Morey's favorite refrain any time I had a deadline that required me to work extra hours.

"Okay, I know. I'll try harder. I'm sorry. Of course I love you. I'll do better next time," I would reply, trying my best to be a good caregiver and wife without rocking the boat.

As the days and years wore on, my body tightened up. After five years, my muscles had atrophied from lack of use since there was never time for exercise or recreation. The pressure to please was compressing me from within, and I felt disconnected from my creative flow of wisdom. I hadn't thought about dancing in years and didn't move my body in any expressive way. This lack of movement stifled my ability to view my situation from a grounded perspective.

I often sat in silence as Morey piled on his list of grievances, feeling myself dissociate from my body. Even though Morey's responses seemed dramatic, some of his complaints felt true, and I latched on to that. Deep down, I knew he was right. I wasn't in love with him, and I felt bad about that even though I didn't want to see him suffer. Afraid to consider the alternative, I tried to convince Morey—and myself—that I was fully committed to making this situation work. I figured that maybe his condition, whatever it was, contributed to his outbursts, and I was willing to give him the benefit of the doubt. It never occurred to me that I could talk back to him or challenge his assumptions, much less offer alternatives to full-time caregiving. And I regretted that I'd jumped into our marriage so quickly. Had my conservative religious views led me astray? Where was God now when I needed him?

4

Plan B

After juggling caring for Morey and working full-time for over five years, a milestone birthday was approaching, my thirtieth, and the years of managing working from home and caring for Morey had caught up to me. As the big day approached, I wanted to relive my teenage years and dance. Getting married so young, I'd missed many milestones of youth. I hadn't danced at the clubs, hung out with the girls for more than a few minutes, or taken time to make mistakes and learn who I was as a person. I was determined to celebrate this birthday in a grand way. The idea of having something to look forward to brought some life back into my flagging body and spirit, and I felt butterflies of excitement. This would be my grand day!

My brother Richard and sister Rose planned to visit from Colorado so we could celebrate my special day. I'd only seen them a few times since getting married, and I hadn't been able to attend my brother's wedding due to my caregiving responsibilities. I couldn't wait to have a few precious days to explore California with my family.

As I searched the Internet, researching beach venues, private hotel rooms, and local dance clubs, I could feel myself lean into it—it felt so good to dream and imagine a day just for me. I would give myself one special moment with my family and closest friends and have a reprieve from the constant challenges I'd been dealing with. I desperately needed a break, and my thirtieth birthday was the perfect opportunity.

I decided that we'd have a nice dinner in Long Beach and then dance the night away to an '80s cover band at a local dance club. I couldn't wait to dust off my dance shoes, and I dreamed of staying at the hotel across the street so I could really feel like it was a getaway. I talked to the club, secured my name on the table reservations, and made a deposit for a hotel room for me and my family. I invited the twins and told my brother and sister about my plans. My heart felt energized, and I couldn't wait to properly bring in the new decade.

A few weeks before the big event, I got up the courage to share my plans with Morey. "Morey, I wanted to let you know that it's important to me this year to have a special way to celebrate my birthday. Turning thirty feels different, and my family will be in town. I want you to know that I'm exploring some possible activities that I could do with them to make the day memorable, including having a nice dinner and going dancing."

My carefully rehearsed speech did not have the effect I'd hoped. I recognized that there weren't any activities outside the house that Morey could participate in given his disabilities. My fear of his reaction to this plan, knowing he'd feel abandoned and left behind, made it difficult for me to honestly express my feelings or desires. I heard myself tremble and trip over words. But here I was, giving it my best shot.

He looked at me with a blank stare. "You know I can't leave the house, and I *need* you here. What if I have an anxiety attack and you aren't home or can't get home quickly? Knowing you'll be away really makes me uncomfortable." He was clearly aghast that I would even consider an evening away from him.

"But Morey, it's my *birthday*. I really need and want a special evening to celebrate. Of course I want you to join, but I know that's not possible. It's important to me to have this time with my family. Please, can you understand?" *Could he be reasonable?*

"I've told you so many times before that I don't want to know when you aren't going to be here because it gives me anxiety knowing you'll be gone. I'd rather not know your plans, and it would be better if you could do something while I'm asleep so I won't worry while you're gone. But now it feels too late because I know you want to do something outside the house, and that'll cause me anticipation anxiety until the day."

The pressure in my chest began to tighten. Clearly, the possibility of getting away for a nighttime party wasn't landing with him in a good way. Something about his tone made me afraid of what he might do if I followed through. I wanted to speak up, defend myself, and say I was doing what I could, but instead, my body froze as it always did.

Continuing the conversation that evening was futile, so I dropped it. But I didn't drop my plans to have a grand affair. I continued those in the background, not bringing it up to Morey again. I hoped he would forget this encounter and I would make my wishes come true.

On the eve of my thirtieth birthday, all my plans were in place. The reservations were booked, my siblings had arrived and were waiting at a nearby hotel, and my friends were on call. There would be champagne and dancing, and I'd found the perfect pair of three-inch purple strappy shoes with chunky wooden heels that I planned to wear for my night on the town. I couldn't wait to feel free for a few hours. I felt a tinge of guilt that I'd gone against Morey's wishes in continuing my birthday adventure plans, but I felt empowered to finally stick up for myself. I kept telling myself it was reasonable to have one evening to myself, and I doubted that Morey would desperately need me to the point that it would infringe on my plans.

On the evening before my birthday, Morey's anxiety started to heighten. I could see his eyes tracking each time I entered the living room to bring him something. He didn't say much. In fact, the silent treatment was something I had gotten familiar with. But I could tell something was off. His emotions seemed to be simmering below the surface, and I wasn't sure what would happen if they boiled over.

"I'm going to go to bed," I told Morey as I started to make my way to my bedroom.

Morey looked at me with a hopeless expression and said, "I really need you tomorrow. I know it's your birthday, and I hope you'll be here. I'm not feeling well, and I can't handle you leaving. I hope you aren't planning to leave the house while I'm awake tomorrow."

Ugh, here we go again. Getting away for an evening was too good to be true. I began to feel that, once again, Morey's needs would overwhelm any plans I'd made.

"Okay. Don't worry—I don't have any plans," I lied, hoping he would drop it and let me go to sleep.

I was used to lying about my plans. It wasn't that I didn't want to be honest, but Morey couldn't handle it, so I had to be discreet when I wanted to have a moment to myself outside the home. I didn't want to engage in another argument with him over my birthday. Our discussion hadn't gone well a few weeks before, and I didn't anticipate that it would go well now. I couldn't stand being on bad terms with my husband, and I knew his medical ailments were complex. I had tremendous compassion for him and knew it was hard for him. At the same time, I needed a break after five years of caregiving. I believed that was a reasonable request.

Yet as I was alone with my thoughts in my bedroom, I started to feel anxious and worried about what might happen if I went. I was used to conceding to all of Morey's demands, even if they crossed my personal boundaries or made me feel uncomfortable.

Plan B

It was new for me to push back and say no. And even though I could rationally see that going would be understandable, deep down, I was afraid of Morey's reaction and wasn't sure I was strong enough for the verbal storm that would come afterward. Plus, I couldn't stop anticipating that he would call me throughout the evening like he normally did when I was out of the house, which would mess up the lightness and joy I wanted to experience with my friends and family.

Shortly before midnight, I decided to cancel. I texted my family and friends.

Sorry, we aren't going to be able to go dancing. It's too much of a change and I am not sure how Morey will react. I'm sorry. As I sent the texts, I felt the tears well up, my body filled with regret and shame.

I was nervous to see how my friends and family would respond. I hadn't been the most reliable person over the last few years and they were used to it, so I knew they would probably understand. But it didn't take away the sting of embarrassment and burning in my chest. I felt trapped, and at that moment, it seemed as if I would never be able to leave.

It's okay, each of my friends and family members replied without emotion. They knew my life was a constant balancing act, and I knew they wanted to support me in whatever way they could.

I tried to breathe a sigh of relief, but I was disappointed in myself for not having the courage or strength to hold fast and honor the plans I'd made, especially when I thought of my siblings, who had traveled to be with me. Still, I was determined to at least do *something* that felt special.

I texted them: *Let's meet for breakfast instead in Long Beach. I'll send you the location.* And with that, I activated Plan B.

The next morning, I woke up half relieved and half disappointed that my grand adventure wouldn't be realized, and I was even more relieved to see that Morey was still asleep. I got dressed in a new purple blouse, dark denim jeans, and a dangly chain necklace before slipping into my fancy new purple heels. I met my brother Richard, sister Rose, and friends Zoey and Quinn at an Irish pub in Long Beach, where they were already waiting for me to enjoy a champagne brunch. I showed off my special outfit and took pictures with the cardboard characters along the pub, imagining I was making my way through the dance club, and I toasted a new year of life with my special people.

After brunch, we walked along Seal Beach Pier and did some boogie boarding at the nearby beach, a place that had been a source of reprieve for me when I was desperate for a break from caregiving. We made the most of our time together before I made my way back home around noon. Thankfully, Morey was still asleep when I crept back into my bedroom, shimmied out of my birthday finery, and slipped into house clothes to remove any evidence of my illicit celebration. I snuggled with my little dog Maggie for a few minutes—her energy and excitement at seeing me always provided an immediate sweet feeling. I prepared myself for a simple day at home watching TV and playing video games with Morey. But I couldn't ignore a welter of regret for caving to Morey's demands. That feeling mixed with guilt for hiding out and anger at Morey for putting me in this position.

5

A Diagnosis

After that birthday, I felt something shift inside me. I didn't know how, but I knew I was ready to make a change. I opened a new journal, a birthday gift I had given myself, and started to imagine the life I wanted to live one day. Inspired by the colorful spiral-bound notebook with passport images plastered across the front, I pictured myself drinking champagne under the lights of the Eiffel Tower and traveling the world. I closed my eyes and imagined each detail until it was impressed upon my heart. I envisioned myself dancing a new dance in every city I visited, charming all the men with my savoir faire, speaking new languages. I would allow myself to get caught in mishaps in search of adventure. As my eyes opened, words spilled onto the crisp white pages like birthday champagne, capturing every delightful sensory detail that flowed through my pen. I reminded myself that one day, I would make these dreams come true.

For the next month, I revisited this sweet little journal daily, allowing myself a small reprieve from the rote drudgery of caregiving and work. New adventures and explorations poured forth from years of darkness with volcanic force as I imagined myself exploring a new country and dancing my way through life once again. Tingles filled my body, electrifying me with joy. *Was a different life possible?*

Dancing on My Own Two Feet

⁓❧

On a brisk October morning a month after my thirtieth birthday, I finally found a doctor who I hoped could help Morey understand his symptoms. After five years of increasing ailments with no reliable explanation, I was feeling discouraged yet brave. I knew Morey needed in-home care. He also needed a doctor's visit to be properly diagnosed. The years in and out of the ER and running all the conventional tests had not added up to a cure, let alone a medical explanation or diagnosis. With my renewed sense that life was possible, I wasn't ready to give up, even though I knew Morey was no longer willing to seek medical help. After months of searching, I found a doctor who specialized in all things unusual: chronic fatigue syndrome, extreme allergies, autoimmune disorders, and the like. *And* he was willing to make house calls.

I called the doctor's office one morning, excited to set up a home visit, but I was informed by the nurse that an in-office visit was required before home care could be arranged.

Doesn't she realize my husband can't leave the house? How is he supposed to make it to the office first? I was frustrated by the bureaucracy of the medical system, but I wasn't ready to throw in the towel.

Without a proper diagnosis for Morey, I felt confined to living my life at his beck and call, with each day becoming more and more untenable for me. At thirty, I craved the adventure I'd missed out on in my twenties, and deep down, I hadn't given up on my desire to start a family one day. Doing so would mean I'd likely need to leave Morey. If I was honest with myself, I didn't want to have a family with him. (Besides, he'd already indicated he didn't want one at all). I also wanted to see if there could be a potential path to recovery for Morey. I recognized that if I found an explanation for his ailments, it might give me the courage to find a way out for myself, a sort of capstone for my caregiving duties.

What if I go as the patient and convince the doctor to come to my house to treat Morey? Surely, it will be harder to reject me in person if I can provide the proper context for the visit and plea for help. After so many evenings daydreaming with my new journal, the potential taste of freedom on the other side of this prison made me willing to be bold and try something unorthodox.

I took a deep inhale before walking up the two flights of stairs to the doctor's office. Morey didn't know I was making this trip, another white lie to keep the peace. I nervously rubbed my hands together as I waited in the cold, sterile exam room for the doctor to arrive. I allowed myself a moment to celebrate my act of courage—and mild subterfuge—to seek answers in the unconventional.

The doctor interrupted my reverie, barely looking up from his clipboard as he said, "Hello, Jennifer. How can I help you today?" He was tall and slender, middle-aged with a practiced kindness I imagined came from years of meeting patients who had tried everything before seeing him.

Maybe this will work.

"Hello. I know this is a bit out of the ordinary. I'm not here for myself but on behalf of my husband," I started.

"Okay." The doctor put down his clipboard and peered at me, intrigued, as my story poured out in one long stream.

"You see, my husband has been very sick for five years now. He seems allergic to everything. He can't shower regularly. He has allergic attacks every time he leaves the house, which has disabled him to the point of being completely homebound. I walk on eggshells to manage his allergic uprisings, which cause him tremendous anxiety. He is constantly fatigued and unable to care for himself. He depends on me for everything. Despite years of doctor visits and a full workup to evaluate his major organs, we haven't been able to find a proper diagnosis. Please, I know your website says you are willing to make house calls. I am begging you to consider coming to my home to evaluate my husband. I truly believe there is more to his condition and need your help to see what we might be missing." I pleaded my case with deep conviction, knowing I didn't want to leave that office without a "yes."

The doctor paused for a few minutes, actively taking notes and mumbling under his breath in a way I couldn't understand.

"I see," he offered. I wasn't sure if that was a positive or a negative. "Well, you certainly do seem to care about helping your husband. I'm not sure if I'll be able to help, but I'm willing to try. There are several tests that we can run to see if something shows up. I can't guarantee we'll find anything, but we can give it a shot."

Tears started flowing from my eyes as I struggled to respond to just this small shred of hope and kindness. Five years of stress and pressure and research and unanswered questions began to lift. I felt incredibly grateful to have found a kind soul willing to help.

"Thank you," I replied, resisting the urge to stand up and give the doctor a hug.

"Let's schedule a nurse to come out and run some tests, and then I'll plan to make a house call once we have the results. We can go from there. And please take care of yourself. Being a caregiver isn't easy, and it's important for you to prioritize your well-being. Are you and Morey getting the support you need to manage the mental health challenges from chronic illness? I have a referral for a therapist if you both would find it helpful." The doctor handed me a stack of papers with orders for tests and a sticky note with a scribbled name of a local therapist.

I thanked him again and made my way to the reception desk to schedule the home visit. I blotted my eyes with a tissue and found the courage to make my way back to my car feeling incredibly hopeful and somewhat in disbelief.

I did it.

A Diagnosis

⁓❧⤳

A few weeks later, the doorbell rang in our two-bedroom bungalow. I opened the screen door to find the kind doctor himself standing on our porch. He was dressed in black slacks, shiny shoes, and a cardigan. He looked more approachable without the sterile office and white coat.

"Hello, Jennifer. It's nice to see you. I have Morey's test results. May I come in?"

"Yes, please. We've been looking forward to your arrival," I replied as I ushered him into our tiny, darkened living room.

The doctor greeted Morey, who was sitting in the reclining chair where he usually sat. Morey offered his hand with a bit of hope glimmering in his eyes. The doctor and I sat down, and I anxiously awaited the results.

"Morey, it's nice to meet you in person. I have the results of the tests we ran. Would you like to know what's going on inside of you?"

The anticipation was getting to both my husband and me. Of course we wanted to know what was ailing Morey. "Yes, please," he and I replied in unison.

With that, the doctor turned the page in his notebook and handed Morey a long sheet of paper outlining his diagnosis. "It's Lyme disease," he said after a brief pause.

I felt like I wanted to cry and scream at the same time. A tremendous weight fell off my shoulders. After years of effort and testing and trying to figure it out, we finally had an explanation for Morey's random, debilitating symptoms. Yet it wasn't clear to me if the prognosis offered enough hope to get excited about. I wondered, *What if the damage is permanent and Morey will live like this forever? How much longer can I manage in this situation, and what am I willing to do to support him in this next part of his journey?* With a diagnosis in hand, I wanted to dance off into the distance and start living my life.

"Thank you," was all I could offer to the doctor as Morey stood in disbelief. I could only anticipate the same mix of reactions swirling through his brain.

"I'll send in some orders for some medicine that we can try to aggressively treat the condition. I don't have any promises, but at least we know what we're dealing with." With that, the doctor gently shook both our hands and made his way back to his car.

Two months later, I was still processing that we'd received a diagnosis for Morey after five years of medical mystery. In the wake of that relief, I was suddenly aware that I desperately needed a break, and I became bolder and more impulsive in taking action to search for a better life. I'd spent the last few months daydreaming and envisioning that magical trip to Europe, using my birthday journal to log all the adventures I hoped to experience while making note of the logistics.

When I was in my journaling zone, I would search travel websites and pretend to book trips just to imagine how long the flight would be, which hotel piqued my interest, and which sights I couldn't do without. The thought of ringing in the new year in Paris created a swirl of excitement in my heart, and during one of my make-believe travel sessions, I found a ten-day deal to London, Paris, Rome, Florence, and Venice at a bargain price. I contemplated hitting "buy." *What if I just went? Surely, I owe myself a break after so many years of caregiving and a reward for helping Morey find a diagnosis.* As I wrestled with this thought, my stomach turned sideways and upside down with fear and excitement. *Just do it!*

Before I could think about the repercussions, I clicked the "buy" button and purchased two tickets. *Eeek! I'm making this happen*, I thought, both stunned and petrified at my impulsiveness. Exultantly, I phoned my sister Rose, and with a grand flourish, invited her to join me on this adventure. She said yes without hesitation, although I could hear the skepticism in her voice, knowing how many times I'd dropped my grand plans in the past. But she had no idea the internal shift this represented in my relationship with Morey. I was going on that trip.

When I pressed that button to purchase the tickets, I ignored the thoughts about what it would mean to leave Morey alone for ten days when I hadn't left his side for even ten hours over the last five years. I was singularly focused on making my dream come true and fantasized about the magical adventure that lay before me. I was afraid to tell Morey about the trip until it was time to go, so I kept my plans a secret for two weeks, carefully going over my itinerary in detail each day, keeping the dream alive despite my mundane daily struggles with Morey, which continued as I counted down to our departure.

Morey knew me well, and I could tell he sensed something was up. I had been secretly packing and leaving my travel gear in the storage room I used for a makeshift kitchen. Morey rarely visited that room lest his symptoms flare up while I was cooking. I'd also secretly run off to the post office to renew my passport; my short bob haircut and tired eyes made for a less-than-desirable passport photo. But I didn't care. I was going to Europe no matter what. My bags were packed and my passport arrived just in time. I intercepted the mail and neatly tucked my treasure away in the front pocket of the small suitcase I would use for a carry-on.

I went to the living room and sat in the recliner next to Morey, trying to keep his holiday spirit up for Christmas. Maggie was nestled next to him, cuddled in a ball on his lap.

"I know you're leaving me," Morey blurted out of the blue. I felt my face getting hot and panic welled up inside, my heart racing.

"What do you mean?" I replied, trying to keep cool.

"I saw your travel itinerary in the back storage room and a

new passport. Why is there a packed suitcase with your things? What's going on?" he asked.

Oh no. He knows I'm leaving. This wasn't the way I had planned this conversation. How do I deal with this now? I took a moment to think before I responded.

"Yes, I'm going on a trip. I am really burned out and I need time away. Don't worry, I've made a list of all the things needed to take care of you, and I'll make meals for the entire ten days so you'll be taken care of. I desperately need this time for myself, and I'll make it as easy for you as I can." I came clean, hoping he would accept and appreciate the thoughtfulness of my plan.

I'd managed the guilt of leaving by convincing myself that by helping Morey be prepared, he would be okay without me while I was away. But I also braced for a long, angry lecture and a litany of reasons I had to stay, like on my birthday.

"Well, you aren't going anywhere," he said instead, uncannily calm.

"What do you mean?" I was getting worried.

"Not without a passport. You're staying here with me." With that, Morey turned back to the TV as if the situation was settled.

I ran back to the storage room, opened the front pocket of my suitcase, and stared in disbelief. My passport was gone.

"You stole my passport!" I yelled as I made my way back to the living room. "Give it back!" I held my hand out to Morey, demanding the return of my travel document.

"No way," he said, and turned off the TV with a threatening stare.

I ran outside and called my sister. Rose didn't answer, so I left a frantic message and told her what Morey had done. I started to cry in disbelief. My hopeful plans and dreams were quickly dissolving into a nightmare.

When I returned to the house, Morey was pacing back and forth, and the situation felt dangerous. He'd stolen my passport.

What else might he do? I returned to my bedroom, forgetting to bring my phone in with me, and cried into my pillow. An hour later, the doorbell rang. I answered it and found two police officers standing in the doorway.

"Hello, ma'am. Are you Jennifer?" one of the officers asked.

"Yes. How can I help you?" Now I was confused. *Had Morey called the cops on me? Did Morey think I called the cops on him?*

"We received a call for a welfare check from your sister. She didn't hear from you when she tried to call you back. She mentioned that your husband stole your passport and there might be a domestic dispute. Is everyone all right?" The men looked at me concerned, reading my body language to see if I was in danger.

"I'm okay. My husband did steal my passport, and I'm supposed to be going on a trip tomorrow." I kept my voice steady and calm. *What will Morey do now?*

"Sir, do you have the lady's passport? If so, can you return it to her?" One of the officers turned to Morey, who looked just as worried as I was and clearly didn't want to get in trouble.

Morey bashfully stood up from his recliner and went to his room, returning with my passport. He handed it to me somewhat forcefully and nodded at the policemen as if he was ready to concede.

"Okay, ma'am. If you need anything else, please let us know. You both have a good evening." And with that, the police officers left our home.

I slumped into the recliner and the pit in my stomach grew. This situation was becoming too volatile for me. *Would I be able to get away?* I began to understand that the trip to Europe was just the beginning. I would have to find a way to leave.

6

Europe or Bust

The day after Christmas, Rose met me at Los Angeles International Airport (LAX), and we finally boarded the plane to London. Our flight from LAX had been delayed, so we were rerouted from British Airways to Air New Zealand. I didn't care how we got to Europe; I was just ready to *go*. My blood was still racing from what felt like a prison break leaving Morey behind.

He will be okay. I will be okay.

Emotionally, it wasn't easy pulling away from the house. Spending thirty minutes in a taxi making its way through traffic to LAX was arguably the hardest part of the trip. I had spent the prior days cooking all of Morey's favorite foods so he would have enough to eat while I was gone. I had organized a three-ring binder filled with instructions and felt confident that I was leaving him fully prepared to take care of himself. I had given his family and our neighbors some additional notes in case they planned to stop by and check on him. Even so, I nearly turned the taxi around. But I knew deep down that it was best for me to move forward.

"Ladies and gentlemen, thank you for flying with us today. We are ready for takeoff, so please make sure your seat belts are securely fastened and seats are in the upright position." The flight attendant prepared the cabin for departure.

I hadn't flown in years, and I was a nervous flier to begin with. I rested my head on my sister's shoulder as I burned off the adrenaline that had carried me through the last two weeks of preparation. Soon, I crashed and fell asleep. A little over ten hours later, I awoke to the commotion of passengers retrieving their bags ready to deplane.

"Are we here already?" I asked my sister in disbelief that I had slept through the entire flight. The buzz of the engine had lulled me to sleep, and without my 3:00 a.m. alarm rousing me to heat up food for Morey, I awoke well rested.

"Yep, let's go!" she replied with a smile that let me know she was ready to explore. It was nice to finally have a partner in crime.

Rose was five years younger than me and had a renewed zest for life; she'd just broken up with her boyfriend of ten years. Our age difference had made it difficult to connect when we were children. While I threw myself into dance and church and played pseudo-mom to her and my brother, she retreated to a friend's house each afternoon after school. She got the short end of the stick being only seven years old when our parents divorced, and my dad compared us to each other, which I sensed bothered her since she got into trouble while I collected gold stars. But I was thankful to have her with me now to share in this experience.

Rose threw her long dirty-blonde hair into a ponytail and grabbed each of our carry-ons from the overhead compartment with ease as we made our way out of the plane. When we went through customs, the agent gave me the first stamp in my brand-new passport, and we headed for the Underground.

Even though I had only booked the trip a few weeks prior, I had planned all the transportation routes throughout our itinerary. I'd left my cell phone at home so Morey couldn't contact me, and I was ready to navigate with a good old-fashioned paper map. As we stood on the platform waiting for the train to arrive, my sister snapped a picture of me. My short bob haircut was fluttering in the light breeze, and I proudly carried our tickets, ready to head downtown. The gray knee-length wool coat I'd bought just for this trip was keeping me warm, and the camera caught me smiling ear to ear. I was genuinely excited and happy in a way I hadn't been for a very long time.

"It's our first time on the Underground!" I beamed with excitement, trying to hold back tears. Here I was on the other side of the world. I even did a little jig on the subway platform, thinking about standing up to Morey and crossing the pond to make something important to me come true.

I had been to Europe only once before as part of a church mission trip during my gap year after high school when I was eighteen. During that trip, I stayed in Manchester, England, with a host family, and exploration was limited to church services and family-friendly sightseeing. Finding myself in London for the first time as a thirty-year-old woman made me feel like a queen.

We got off the Tube at St. James's Park in the center of Westminster. I looked at my map as we carried our bags up the stairs of the Underground and onto a cold winter street in the center of London. As we turned onto Caxton Street, St. Ermin's Hotel stood before us. I stopped, mesmerized by its late Victorian grandeur.

Windows all around the perimeter twinkled from the warm glow of lights inside, and the hotel was elegantly dressed for Christmas with green garland and red bows lining the brown bricks. I could see a proper Victorian Christmas tree beckoning invitingly through the windows. As we entered the lobby, the warmth of a cozy wood-burning fireplace cut the chill from our fingers and helped us defrost from the bitter outdoors. A large white marble staircase twisted around to the upper levels with dark carpet lining the walkway. I was in awe of its majestic beauty and was thrilled that this was the first stop of our European adventure. As I warmed myself by the blazing fire, something in me that was frozen from all the years with Morey began to melt away. I felt my own internal spark answering the fire and enchantment in this room.

Since it was too early to officially check in, we left our bags at the front desk, reapplied our layers, and, barely defrosted, made our way back onto the London streets. A few blocks away, we heard the bell chime from Big Ben, and as we got closer, a gold palace-like structure glistened in the foreground. I took a minute to let the chimes reverberate throughout my body, offering a healing balm to my spirit. My sister snapped another picture of me as I posed with my hands high in exultation. As we continued our pace, we realized the building before us was the Houses of Parliament, stretching for what seemed to be several blocks. The steeples and spokes that emerged from the golden kingdom took my breath away and I stood with my jaw open for several minutes, gulping in waves of crisp Christmas air.

Snap. Another picture to document the memory. My sister was going to make sure I remembered every bit of this special trip.

"I can't believe we're here. It's magnificent," I said to Rose as she whisked me into a nearby pub for refreshments and to warm up.

We ordered cheeseburgers and pints of beer at Albert's Pub as we watched the locals and tourists come in and out to escape the cold. I felt the years of eating alone slowly melt away with each drink my sister and I shared together. Garlands framed the edge of the pub like a warm sweater and Christmas music played in the background. My sister and I raised our glasses.

"Cheers to the beginning of a two-week adventure. May all your dreams come true," my sister toasted. We sipped the bubbly amber brew. I wasn't normally a beer drinker, but I felt sophisticated toasting pints with my sister.

Several hours and more than a few pints later, we finally were able to check into our room. The floors creaked as we carried our bags out of the small elevator, which barely fit one person at a time. Before we could change into our pajamas, we both crashed on our respective twin beds and fell asleep, trying to ignore the heartburn that was bubbling beneath the surface from too much ale.

It took a few days to adjust to the time change, and Rose and I kept waking up in the middle of the night. We watched *The Sound of Music* and any other American movie that was on TV during the predawn hours, not quite ready to fully embrace the local British channels. We meticulously arrived at breakfast right as it opened at 6:00 a.m., hungry for scones and hot tea. We tried creamy scrambled eggs and blood sausage (only once). But mostly, we napped between short bursts of consciousness as the upstairs guests walked above us, causing more creaking throughout our hotel room. My body and mind needed rest after so many years of being pulled in multiple directions.

During our waking hours, we visited all the sights we could. We cast my planners and carefully jotted notes aside and catered to our own internal rhythms and desires, something I realized I'd never done before this trip. We toured Westminster Abbey, saw *Wicked* in the West End, watched the changing of the guard at Buckingham Palace, looked down on the city from the London Eye, waltzed through Hyde Park in the rain, and made our way into Harrods to escape the misty weather. On our last day in London, we finished in classic fashion with afternoon tea in our hotel lobby. We had become experts at adding cream to our English breakfast tea in just the right way and taking our scones, fresh from the oven, with clotted cream. We split the little tea sandwiches of cucumber and egg in half, each of us getting an equal share. We delighted in listening to children speak with British accents. It felt comforting to bond with my sister and share such special moments together. I realized that living within Morey's universe meant I hadn't been able to develop relationships with my family or friends, and that made me long for more connections with others.

"Jennifer, it's so nice to see you smile again," Rose said on our last night in London.

I was surprised by this comment, not realizing the weight that I had been carrying was so physically visible.

"I've missed you. It's been so wonderful to be a part of this journey together. Thank you for inviting me on this trip," Rose continued. Her easygoing spirit, her desire to be supportive, and her willingness to go with the flow throughout our adventures meant more to me than I realized. I needed a safe person to help me ease out of my rigid life and find a more natural balance, and she didn't pressure me to do more than I was ready for. I realized this was the first time I was really getting to know her—I hadn't done that during childhood. Being able to spend time with her and experience new adventures together made my heart warm.

Yet I was embarrassed to admit that I rarely thought of Morey during our time in London. Being in a different country and time zone allowed my brain and body to completely transform into an adventurer, and I didn't want to be reminded of my life back home. I had sent him an email to let him know we arrived, but he didn't respond—which was unlike his constant calls when I was at home. Beyond that gesture, I had otherwise forgotten my home life and obligations. *That's part of the point*, I reminded myself. I felt free and light, and with wide eyes, I eagerly absorbed each new experience, soaking everything in, like the English trifle sponges we'd eaten with our latest meal. I was determined to drink in all the sweetness (and ale) the city had to offer. Years of exhaustion and ignoring my own needs were fading with each day, and I focused on the pleasures of travel before me.

After four nights in London, on the night before New Year's Eve, my sister and I were ready to make one of my childhood dreams come true. As our train made the two-hour journey from London to Paris under the English Channel, I couldn't stop smiling. I was on my way to France! I'd dreamed of this since I was a little girl, long before I set foot in California, and I was about to put my French to the test. As the hills passed, I felt an ease that I hadn't known before. While the French countryside played across the window and Taylor Swift's "Fearless" played on my iPod, I laughed and giggled like a giddy child reconnecting with the world after emerging from a well-kept hideout in a game of hide-and-seek.

Yet when the train finally came to a stop at the Gare Du Nord station, I was horrified. Graffiti lined the walls and threatening figures loomed behind the station's dark corners, seemingly ready to prey on whoever might be foolish enough to be their next victim. I ran to the station bathroom to catch my bearings and plot our next destination, but I couldn't figure out how to use the coin machine at the entrance.

"*Ne marche pas,*" I said to the nearby attendant as I pointed to the broken machine.

I kept my guard up in the metro as we made our way to our hotel in the 14th arrondissement, not too far from the Eiffel Tower—or so I thought. After dropping off our bags, we grabbed a sandwich at the kebab café next door, and I sent Morey a quick email from an Internet café across the street to let him know I'd arrived.

Made it to France. Hope you are doing well. Love you. Bye. I clicked "send" and returned to my sister. The link between Morey and me faded further with each cursory check-in.

A few minutes later, we emerged from the metro again, this time right in front of the Louvre. We watched cars swish through the roundabout in front of the triangle of glass that emerged from the center of a courtyard, reminding me of Egypt's Great Pyramids.

Snap. This time *I* took a photograph, capturing the swirling cars and their lights twinkling around us. I felt my own sparkle greet the energy of the Parisian streets. I enjoyed this exploration.

The sun was starting to set, and the Louvre and accompanying buildings lit up in blue, yellow, and gold from every angle. The crowds had dissipated since the museum was closed for the day. A gentle rain started to fall and I opened my purple umbrella, inhaling the delicious scent of ozone in the crisp air. I wasn't going to let a little sprinkle get in the way of our Paris adventure. As I turned my gaze to the left, I saw another monument sparkling in the distance, shimmering with silver and gold, like diamonds dressing a movie star. Of course she was sparkling—*the Eiffel Tower.*

"Let's walk there," I suggested to my sister as if the *Tour Eiffel* was just down the block.

"Walk? It looks *really* far away," she replied, trying to gauge the distance and my motivations. Rose knew once I set my mind on something I tended to go for it, whatever the cost.

Her protestations were useless. I had already started skipping off in the direction of my love, ready to embrace her. Nearly an hour later, that light romantic mist had turned into a frigid, drenching downpour, chilling us to the bone in our lightweight raincoats, and it seemed as if we were still miles from our destination. I could feel blisters accumulating on my feet and I wasn't sure I could walk any farther.

"Can I trade shoes with you?" I asked Rose, desperate for a reprieve from my swollen ankles. I regretted the decision to walk, realizing the metro would have been a saner choice.

"Uh, okay. Sure, sis, whatever you want." And with that, Rose removed her size ten Adidas and handed them to me. In exchange, I offered a pair of size nine boots, and we continued toward our destination. I appreciated my sister's easygoing nature now more than ever.

Swapping shoes felt like a ritual, like putting on my pointe shoes for the first time in ballet class, only this time, instead of feeling constricted, I felt free. Literally stepping into my sister's shoes helped unlock a bit of that unattached, carefree attitude she still had as she lived life on her own terms in her twenties. I wanted to feel that as much as I could on this trip. I did a little twirl as we continued our quest toward Her Majesty.

A few moments later, my cheeks hurt from smiling so broadly. (When was the last time I'd smiled like that?) It didn't matter that I could barely feel my hands, or that my toes were numb from the cold and wet, or that wearing my sister's too-big shoes in a January rain was causing chafing and blisters I would regret later. The sparkling lights of the Eiffel Tower made up for all that, warming me from within. It was quieter than I imagined for the day before New Year's Eve. *Maybe the French are more civilized than I thought.*

From the base of the tower, with the lights of Paris surrounding me, I raised a bottle of cheap champagne to my mouth. My sister and I had gotten it by negotiating with a haggler trying to take advantage of tourists. I took a sip, the lukewarm bubbles healing me from the inside. *We made it.* I couldn't believe the long, winding path we'd taken to get here. But we made it.

I stopped suddenly, realizing I was an ocean and a full continent away from my caregiver life with Morey. Only a few months after writing in my dream journal and tossing my desire to see the Eiffel Tower into the universe, I was here at her feet, experiencing the beginning of a new year with my sister in the City of Lights. There, in the meadow at the base of the tower, drinking cheap (but rather good) French champagne, laughing with my sister, I made a promise that this was finally, truly the beginning of a new chapter in my life. At that moment, I knew there was no way back. I might return to California, but I could not—would not—return to the status quo when I made my way back to Morey and the West Coast.

A week later, after a whirlwind tour of Italy, a bad cold, and a twenty-six-hour journey home, I stood in front of the door, dreading Morey's response to my arrival. But I couldn't run away forever, so I opened the door to my home and looked around. Morey wasn't in his familiar recliner, and our house was too small to hide in. *Did something happen to him? Maybe he's just in the bathroom. Good. I have a few minutes to breathe before I face him.*

Morey came into the living room as I was putting down my bags.

"Did you have a good time?" he asked with a coldness that didn't make me want to respond.

"I did, thank you," I replied, trying not to cough. My eyes were bloodshot, and I desperately needed a shower.

What I wanted to say was, "Actually, it was the best time of my life, and I can't wait to go back." Wisely, I realized that might not go over well, so I stuck with the basics.

"Good. Look, I'm not doing well, and I really need you now that you are home. Can you help make me some food? I haven't eaten in days." Morey turned his attention to the television.

Visibly distraught and defeated, my natural tendency to worry kicking into high gear and erasing half the joy of my trip, I went to the kitchen and opened the refrigerator. Inside were all the meals I'd made before I left, untouched. I stood with my mouth open for what felt like an eternity, trying to reconcile what had happened.

"Why didn't you eat any of the meals I left for you?" I was in shock.

"They didn't sound good," Morey replied casually.

I screamed inside, *They didn't sound good?* So, all my effort and worry and anxiety about how he would survive without me was in vain? With that, I realized that Morey had found a way to fend for himself while I was gone, despite my best efforts to take care of him. I realized, perhaps for the first time, that I had a choice about whether I stayed.

7

Goodbye
to All That

A week after returning from my trip, I was back to my old routine with Morey. But I couldn't shake the realization that my chronically ill husband had survived without me while I was away. I wondered if I would be able to live without him if I tried. Even though I felt strong when I was five thousand miles away, all the pressures and obligations and residual guilt from being away returned whenever I thought of leaving.

How does someone in good faith leave a spouse so disabled and dependent? What will people think? Who will take care of him?

But my glimpse of a life so different from the one I was living kept coming back to me. I looked through the stack of papers Morey's doctor had given me when I visited him in his office that first day, begging for help. There I found the yellow sticky note with the name of a local therapist penciled in. I stared at the number for quite a few minutes until I finally got up the courage to dial.

"Hello, this is Dan. How can I help you?" He answered on the first ring.

Oh no. I was hoping to leave a message.

"Uh, hi. My name is Jennifer, and I got your name from my husband's doctor. You see, my husband has been disabled for many years and I'm looking for some support to help me navigate my life as a caregiver. I was hoping you could help." There—I'd asked for help. It was a start. I would need help navigating any potential changes because I was too scared to try it on my own. And I reminded myself that asking Mandy for help early in my career had opened up more creative possibilities than I could have imagined. I was ready to give it a shot.

"I would be happy to help. How does next Friday look for you? Say, two p.m.?" I could tell Dan was already penciling me in on his calendar.

"Uh, okay. I can make that work," I agreed, recognizing that Morey would most likely be asleep and I could sneak away to meet Dan at his office in hopes of gaining the courage to explore my options.

In the weeks that followed, and as our ten-year wedding anniversary approached, tensions were high. Morey was upset again—over what, exactly, it wasn't clear. I had started the day excited to receive a spot bonus from my manager, a thank-you for the late nights and weekends I had been working to meet our deadlines. I was looking forward to cashing in my prize for some time at the spa—something I desperately needed after splitting my time between work and caregiving. But Morey wouldn't have it. It seemed like he trampled anything that brought me joy.

"Save it," he insisted. "You don't need to waste money on the spa or on yourself. It's better to save it for later."

I was puzzled that he had such a strong opinion on how I spent my money since I was the main one in the home earning any. I was self-aware enough to recognize that my mental health was reaching a breaking point, but I still felt a swarm of guilt amid the need to comply with his wishes. It was only recently—and with the help of my new therapist—that I'd begun to think about not just whether Morey was okay but also if *I* was okay.

Working with Dan and his gentle demeanor had provided me a safe space to question whether my concerns were valid, and each week, I felt the string of guilt loosen as I walked out his doors.

As Morey continued to harp on the need for me to save the bonus, my conflict between caring for him and caring for myself made me feel like I was splitting in two. I rocked in the chair next to Morey while the TV murmured in the background. My mind was racing. I was ashamed to admit that I'd started to believe his lies again: I wasn't good enough, wasn't deserving of spending money on myself, and no one would love me the way Morey did if I left. Morey liked to remind me of these "truths" at any chance he could. In therapy, I was learning to question whether I should believe them.

My body felt like it was failing, and I started to worry that if I didn't do something soon, I wouldn't be around much longer. The damage from years of living in an unhealthy relationship had finally caught up with me. Even thinking about leaving caused the inflammation to return. The fire in my belly intensified and the anxious energy flowed through my veins. I felt that my body was trying to tell me something, and I needed to listen. What if my inner wisdom was screaming from my bowels and I didn't have the courage to act? *Am I really worthy, and is this situation really that bad?*

Yes, it is. But I was not convinced.

My mind continued to pivot between feeling strong and feeling unsure. I felt like I was doing multiple pirouettes on repeat, unable to stop or find stable ground. My mind felt dizzy, and I was losing focus on my center. As my mind continued to spin, I imagined myself as a wildflower, free and flowing in the breeze. Could that flower break free of the roots of obligation and take shape in my being to help bring color back into my life?

Meanwhile, Morey returned to his steady state of playing video games in the seat next to me. Yet the ongoing conflict in my mind was becoming too much, and I felt the urge to leave. I walked out the back door into the sunlight, hoping the fresh air would settle my brain. But instead of calming down, I became more worked up. I walked through the tall grass in the yard, sifting my hands through the tips, and collapsed without thought in the back corner. I lost control of my hands and felt disconnected from my rational side. Before I could fully comprehend what was happening, I found myself uncontrollably hitting my head with my hands in frustration. I was doing it so hard that I nearly passed out, my temples throbbing and bruised. I was lost in a dance I hadn't chosen, and my body, which had so long ago responded to my every command, was now taking its own course without me. I was literally losing my mind, and I was scared to be expressing self-harm.

My mind flashed uncontrollably over memories of the last five years, black-and-white images appearing as if they were scenes from an old silent film. Days of waking in the dark and making Morcy's meals, poring over medical manuals, the constant balance of sneaking out of the house to do chores, running to the Laundromat, and cooking in the dank storage room. Trying not to disturb Morey, sitting by him in the dark as he ran through his anxiety cycle. Hiding my comings and goings, living in fear of his reaction and the mental bruising that would follow. A dark gloom pressed down on me as if I had lived through five years of caregiving on rainy days with no sunshine in sight, even though it had been sunny nearly every day in Southern California. I wanted to unplug the movie projector and throw it out the window of my brain, but the images wouldn't stop coming. I was having a breakdown.

How could I have gotten to this emotional state? I asked myself with the part of my brain that was observing as my mind, body, and emotions crashed down on me. I was unable to find a suitable answer. My heart beat uncontrollably, and for the first time, I was really scared. The pain in my gut continued to intensify and spread through the rest of my body like a cancer feeding on flesh, causing me to cry out in sorrow, although I was pretty sure no one could hear me. I was also sure no one would rescue me from my desperation even if they could. I looked up at the wooden fence next to me, cracked and in need of a good stain, feeling like I was in a prison and searching for my escape.

I took a deep breath and put my hands on my heart, my vehicle for love and human connection, the source of my power for hope and transformation. With Dan's encouragement, I'd recently started to embrace mindfulness by doing yoga at home in my small moments of free time, and my online instructor focused on connecting with the heart center.

"What are you trying to tell me?" I whispered to myself. "I'm listening."

After a brief pause, I pulled myself up from the ground, wiped the dirt off my tattered shorts, and walked back into the house, passing the kitchen and into my bedroom, closing the door behind me. I collapsed onto my bed and closed my eyes.

The doubts started tap-dancing through my mind again, and I felt helpless to shut them down. *Can I really be strong enough to walk away? Can I really survive starting over and heal the trauma that's now fully coming to life? Am I a bad person for leaving? What will my life look like five years from now if I don't make a change?* I knew what I needed to do, but would I have the courage to do it? Or would I get stuck again in this sad waltz that seemed to hold me fast in its firm embrace?

The next morning, I woke unrefreshed, my head and heart still buzzing from the trauma of the previous day. I spent the morning perusing old journals, looking for a sanity check to see if I was overreacting to Morey's outbursts over how I spent my spot bonus. Yesterday's experience had scared me, and it was the first time my body had felt so much pain that it lingered into the next day. My eyes were swollen from sobbing throughout the night. My heart felt like it had been ripped out of my chest and was lying on the ground in the hot sun, vulnerable and naked. My adrenal glands felt shriveled, and my body craved rest.

The seeds of doubt started to fill my mind again as I wondered if I had been too sensitive the day before. *Am I the crazy person?* I wondered. I wasn't sure anymore.

Except, I was sure. Reading my journals, I could see in my heart that I'd been on a journey to leave this unhealthy marriage since my thirtieth birthday, over six months earlier. The path to this moment had not been a smooth, gliding waltz but a jagged-edged cha-cha—two steps forward, one back. Yet there was no doubt my body was telling me I could no longer dance this dance.

Please don't let me talk myself out of leaving, I pleaded to myself. I needed encouragement and courage to push me forward in hopes of preserving the mental capacity and physical health that I had left. I had reached my limit. The situation with Morey was precarious, and I knew I'd have to proceed cautiously if I was going to walk away. One wrong step and he would realize I was leaving. I was scared to think what might happen next.

I started preparing in advance of my eventual departure. First, I knew I needed to find a safe haven where I could stay when things inevitably erupted. I had recently started taking therapeutic drives through Seal Beach, the community where I'd chosen to celebrate my thirtieth birthday. When I saw a "for rent" sign in front of a single-story complex of bungalow apartments just two blocks from the beach, I immediately called the number. The price was right, and I signed a one-year lease.

Dancing on My Own Two Feet

Only a ten-minute drive from my house, Seal Beach was one of the few places I could retreat to during the darkest nights of living with Morey. I looked forward to the majestic sunsets overlooking Catalina Island with the Seal Beach Pier lit up in the background, and I'd spent many nights sitting on a hill of sand watching the ocean waves dance along the shoreline, a much-needed sense of calm washing over my chaotic mind. I would peruse the tiny little main street dotted with local eateries and boutique shops, offering an old-school California lifestyle that was becoming harder and harder to find. I wondered if God was finally helping me see the light out of my darkness.

Over the next month, I secretly and deliberately made the little gem of an apartment into a home. Furtively sneaking out when Morey was asleep, I made my way to every discount store I could find to furnish my new refuge. Pale blue dishes from the dollar store accented a light blue couch I found on clearance at a discount furniture superstore. On weekends, I snuck off to assemble a white bookcase, a writing desk, a taupe entertainment center, and a twin mattress set I found at the local Big Lots. The physical labor of assembling furniture started to bring fresh blood into my veins, helping me find moments of clarity and peace that I was headed in the right direction. After getting a joint checking account when we got married in our early twenties, we hadn't considered opening individual accounts and I knew that any suspicious amount or large purchase would spark red flags for Morey, so I tried to keep the costs low. Separate accounts hadn't seemed necessary at the time, but now that decision was wreaking havoc on my ability to keep my plans a secret.

Morey called one day when I was on my way home from my weekly therapy session with Dan. "We have a problem," he said a few days after what I thought had been careful purchases for my new apartment. He sounded frantic. "I think someone stole our credit card. There are several hundred-dollar purchases from a furniture store, and I don't see any new furniture," he continued.

"Uh . . . oh yeah, that. I'm familiar with those purchases," I quickly replied. "I was thinking of upgrading some of our home furniture. It just hasn't arrived yet." I'd shared this act of self-preservation with Dan and tried to process the guilt from my desire to withhold the truth. I knew it wasn't right, but I was trying to keep the peace for as long as I could.

"Hmmm. Okay," Morey said. "Well, I just wanted to make sure it wasn't fraudulent." He didn't sound convinced.

After that conversation, I knew things were getting too transparent. I needed to move some money into a separate account, and I needed to get a new credit card for the inevitable day when I left the house. I was our household's sole wage earner and didn't want to leave Morey without a way to support himself, an offering to assuage my dwindling guilt. Morey was wise and had tremendous street smarts from his independent upbringing. I knew he would be canny in a split.

That afternoon, I went to my local bank and opened new bank and credit card accounts in my own name, the first separate accounts I'd had since getting married nearly a decade earlier. I transferred money from our joint account so I would have a buffer before I could transfer my paychecks to the new account. I knew there wouldn't be much time before Morey realized the money was gone. I needed to act swiftly. In the days that followed, while Morey was preoccupied with video games or taking a nap, I started secretly packing my clothes and transferring them in small batches to my car, anticipating my eventual departure.

One sunny summer evening in early June 2010, Morey seemed on edge after dinner. He was still suspicious after our call about the odd charges on our credit card a few weeks prior. That evening, he began to follow me around the house, pounding his fist on the counter and raising his voice in a way that jangled my nerves. Though we'd had many fights, intimidating arguments, manipulations, and silent treatments, this was the first time Morey got physical when I didn't respond as he wanted. I retreated to my bedroom—usually a place of safety and privacy—and Morey followed closely behind me. He marched in and opened the closet door, then stood in shock when he saw it was empty.

"Where are all your things?" he screamed.

"Uh . . . in my car, just in case," I replied without thinking, trembling in fear.

"Just in case what?" he continued in disbelief as the dots started to connect in his head.

How do I respond now? My mind was spinning and my heart was racing. I hadn't thought carefully about what to say at this moment. In my plan, it all went very differently. But I also knew this was the time to be brave. I could no longer tolerate apathetically standing still or allow myself to be paralyzed by his trance. I needed to stick up for myself.

"I think it's time for me to move on," I replied, the words finding their way to my lips.

"Move on?!" It was clear Morey could sense his control and power slipping away. Perhaps he'd thought this could happen, but when confronted with the actual threat of change, all his anger came out. He moved to the bedroom door, locked it, and hovered over me threateningly.

This is it, I thought. I had seen too many Lifetime movies and knew this was not headed in a direction that would end well. It was the first time I feared for my physical safety. I had gotten used to the verbal and emotional attacks, but I was in uncharted territory with physical intimidation. I could hear a distressed Maggie barking from the foot of the bed, and I felt her trying to protect me.

The adrenaline rushed through my veins, and I could feel my heart beating through my chest. Morey's chiseled cheeks were so close to mine that I could see micro scars from shaving blunders. A balloon of courage filled within me. *This is my moment to leave.* My instincts took over. I pushed my way past Morey, unlocked the bedroom door, grabbed my purse, ran through the back door, and hopped into my car before the screen door even had a chance to slam shut. I quickly reversed my car down the long driveway and made my way through the empty streets, trying to calm myself down.

"I made it," I whispered to myself, trying to lower my heart rate. I recognized that I was lucky and things could have been much worse, given how quickly the situation was escalating.

My phone kept buzzing and Morey's messages piled up in my voicemail as I made my way south onto the dark 405 Freeway. I didn't pick up the phone. It took everything within me to stay focused on the road with the blur of streetlights and passing cars vying for my attention.

"You can do this," I kept repeating to myself as I turned off the freeway and onto the Pacific Coast Highway. Just a few more miles and I would be safe.

As I pulled into the back alley of the Seal Beach bungalow, I took a deep breath and settled my soul before making the one-minute walk to my new front door. Bright blue and purple hydrangea flowers lined the path, and I could taste the salty ocean air. The stars were starting to shine, and the cool mist welcomed me with open arms.

I can do this. I placed the key into the lock and turned the doorknob. I flicked on the light, locked the door, and embraced my new surroundings, heaving a big sigh of relief. I was home.

The next morning, the sun started to peek through the sheer purple window shades I had hastily hung a few weeks earlier, a furtive purchase on the old credit card that Morey hadn't noticed.

I could hear birds chirping in the distance and caught a glimpse of seagulls making their way to the boardwalk as the morning light started to shine in. It took me a moment to realize where I was, the newness of my surroundings yet to fully sink in. For a minute, I let myself bask in the sense of peace that overwhelmed me.

I couldn't believe I had done it. I'd actually left. I was free. I turned on my cell phone, which I had buried under my pillow the night before, hoping to forget my messy escape. The phone's buzzing jolted me back to reality.

Where are you?
When are you coming back?
What is happening?
Why are you so mad?
How could you abandon me?
I need *YOU!!!!!*

Texts from Morey had piled up overnight while I relished my peace. It was clear that he expected me to return. I immediately started to question whether I'd made the right decision and wondered if my recollection of the relationship was built on false pretense. The doubts flooded in, washing over me in waves.

Had I overreacted? Was my version of reality accurate? *Yes*, I reminded myself. *It had to be.*

I felt bad for leaving Morey behind, but the serenity that met me that morning was too sweet not to savor. I closed my eyes and returned to my bed, closing the window shades and placing the pillow over my eyes to keep the sunlight out. I wasn't quite ready to face the reality of the day, and I wanted time to imagine a different life for myself.

I allowed myself a minute to dream. I felt goose bumps as I acknowledged how deeply I longed for new experiences and adventure. After feeling like a prisoner in my own life for so long, I wanted to see the world again and go back to Europe. I wanted to dance again. I wanted to figure out who I was and what was important to me. There was so much to learn about what I really wanted—so much that I hadn't had a chance to explore as an adult. *Was it really possible to make my youthful dreams of dancing around the world a reality?*

As I lay in bed, the sound of the gulls and the salt of the Pacific air in the background, I allowed myself to envision the life I would have one day. A life of love, dance, children, and adventures. Sipping (better) champagne in Paris, frolicking in the cobblestone streets of Venice with someone I loved, and dancing the waltz in Vienna. I couldn't wait to get started, but my heart tugged and tightened at the thought of making these dreams a reality. As much as I longed for freedom, it felt fragile and delicate, like a newborn baby with a soft spot and a weak neck that needed delicate care and support to avoid injury. My heart had been bruised by past experience, and I was hesitant to risk it being trampled. The thought of leaving my disabled spouse for good brought on a subtle sense of guilt and that familiar pit in my stomach, cramped with unease. I knew I needed time to navigate my conflicting emotions to find a safe way forward.

A few hours later, armed with a bolt of courage to start a new chapter, I left my apartment and made my way onto Main Street. Each step I took toward the ocean brought a greater sense of calm. I realized I had barely eaten since I'd left home and stopped at a charming pizza joint near the boardwalk. As I dove into the chewy goodness of a perfectly reheated New York–style slice, with crusty edges and cheese oozing off my plate, I savored the moment and resisted the urge to check my phone. For so long, I had been a victim of the ever-present anxiety of anticipating when Morey would need me. But now, seated alone in a big booth with a red-and-white checkered tablecloth, I was finally able to relax in peace. I felt my mind and body release from the constant anticipation of Morey's calls. They hungered for healing, and I knew I was not going back. I didn't want to second-guess my decisions anymore, and I wanted to feel confident in my abilities. But living in the in-between phase was uncomfortable. Surely, I would have to face Morey at some point. But I didn't have to do it today. Today, I would eat pizza on the beach and allow my energy to recharge with the freshness of the sea breeze.

I have so much to offer.

I will have my life back.

With each affirmation, the ties of loyalty and obligation that bound me to my past began to dissolve.

8

This Ain't
the Movies, Kid

In the days after I left Morey, I found that healing and shifting a life entangled with others' lives wasn't so easy. For the first week, I struggled to get out of bed almost every day without feeling deep fear and vulnerability for leaving Morey. *What have I done? Will he find me? Did I make a mistake? Is he okay?* These thoughts haunted me each night as I tried to sleep, and I felt like I was completely naked on a jagged rock balancing in the middle of the ocean. In these moments, I spent time journaling my feelings at my new writing desk and tried to remind myself of my independence each time I placed those pale blue dollar store dishes back in the cabinet.

I was willing to empty my bank account for a chance to find myself again and live. But living alone was far from the joyful adventure I had imagined, and it brought its own form of struggle. Prior to my twilight marriage with Morey, I had known almost no life beyond taking care of my family. I found it hard to make decisions or trust my instincts. I hadn't realized how much my self-confidence had suffered; I was always second-guessing myself from the trauma of making every decision under constant surveillance.

Should I spend money on new clothes or time with friends? Do I like this piece of furniture? Can I afford it? Is it okay to go by plane and see my family? What if Morey needs me again and I'm not there?

The thoughts were endless. For the first few weeks, I still visited Morey periodically to assuage my worry and guilt, providing home-cooked meals and light cleaning to assure myself he was okay. It was hard for me to let go of the part of me that needed to be his caregiver, and I needed to know that he was okay before I could really allow myself to move on. And I still wasn't sure who I was without this person to help and care for.

The first time I visited Morey after I left him, it felt like going to a stranger's house when I hadn't been invited. I used my key to open the back door, and Maggie came running toward me. She licked my face with a million kisses and was so excited to see me.

"Hi, Morey. It's Jenn. I'm coming to see how you're doing." There was no response.

I grabbed Maggie in my arms and walked into the living room. Morey was absorbed in his video games and didn't acknowledge my arrival.

"Okay," I said. "I'm going to make a few meals for you to get you through the week." I opened the refrigerator, which was still full of the meals I'd made the week before I left.

Why isn't he eating any of the food I'm making? I felt like I was going crazy, and the silent treatment was driving me nuts. It seemed Morey's treatment plan wasn't making a big difference in his symptoms. So, I threw a few more basic meals together in the makeshift kitchen, adding them to the growing pile in the fridge. I kissed Maggie and put her down, trying not to catch her in the door as I prepared to leave.

"Okay, I'm leaving. I'll come back in a few days and check on you again. Bye." Again, my statement was met with silence.

I felt better knowing Morey was still alive and was somehow managing to take care of himself, but I was annoyed that he didn't appreciate my efforts to help him and he wasn't eating the food I'd made. It felt manipulative. I think I wanted him to honor the sacrifices I had made for so many years and the good intent

I'd had in taking care of him for so long. External validation was a mechanism for me to evaluate my self-worth, and it was hard to feel rejected. But what did I expect? I tried to remind myself why I left.

I returned two weeks later, feeling proud of myself for making it an extra week before my visit. It was like I was weaning off an addictive drug and it took time for the poison to get out of my system. My therapy sessions with Dan and talks with my friends and family helped me realize that I was on the path to recovery and it was okay to walk away for good.

"It's me again," I said, coming through the back door once more.

This time, Morey was in the kitchen.

"I don't know why you keep coming here. Every time you come back, it's like a knife in my chest. I'm not doing well. I'm still very sick, and you left me. I hope you're happy with yourself."

I hadn't expected a confrontation and hadn't mentally prepared myself for this conversation. I stood in shock as he stared me down, my heart starting to race. "Uh, okay. Well, I don't have to come back. I was just trying to make sure you were okay. I know you don't have a lot of support, and I'm sure it's not easy navigating this on your own." I tried my best to respond by being empathetic to his situation and trying to keep the peace.

He raised his voice. "You're right. *It's not* easy."

I felt vulnerable and afraid and remembered how things had escalated so quickly the night I finally left. I didn't want a repeat situation.

"Okay. I'm leaving." Internally, I started to accept that my work was done.

"Whatever. Bye." Morey made his way back into the living room as if he was indifferent to my coming or going.

I felt an inner strength fill me from inside. The small steps I had made to honor my needs had fueled me, and my friends and family members' acknowledgment that the situation was no longer good for me rang in my head. I looked Maggie in the eyes, her little body twirling in circles in front of me as tears rolled down my cheeks. She was the one who was hardest to leave, my honorary daughter who had comforted me each night. I gave her a big hug and whispered in her ear, "Goodbye."

As I walked out the back door, I felt a mix of relief and sadness. Relief that I wouldn't have to deal with Morey's manipulation and guilt-tripping anymore but sadness that our relationship had come to this. I knew it wasn't healthy for either of us, but it still hurt to let go of someone I had cared about for so long. As I got into my car and drove away, I felt a weight lift off my shoulders. I was finally free from the constant stress and anxiety that had consumed my life for so long. It was time to focus on my own healing and happiness. I knew it wouldn't be easy, but I took a deep breath and reminded myself that I had made the right decision. I reversed my car down the driveway without looking back. I never saw Morey or Maggie again.

9

Sky Full of Butterflies

Six months after leaving Morey, I dug my heels into the cold sand as I watched the sky change colors in front of me, this time from a different continent. It was my first solo adventure abroad traveling as a single woman. I didn't want to miss out on a chance to see the world, so when an opportunity came up with my accounting firm to travel to Australia and the Great Barrier Reef exactly one year after my grand European adventure with Rose—which had been the beginning of everything new—I jumped at the chance to flex my newfound independence.

Since none of my friends or family were able to make it this time, I was adventurous and booked the most creative hotel I could find to enjoy after my business meetings were done. That's how I found myself peering out the window of a small propeller plane and gazing down on a sea of green as I and a few other adventurers were ferried from Brisbane to Bargara Beach, Australia. The flight attendant made her way down the aisle offering a complimentary light snack and a cocktail. I was surprised to find that Down Under, even on this little prop plane, the amenities were excellent. After a short hop, the plane made a screeching halt on a too-short runway and I took a deep breath, ready for some magical adventures.

Driving through the town of Bargara Beach barely took a few minutes. There was a small grocery store offering a few provisions for tourists, but not much else. I stepped out of my cab and inhaled a giant gulp of humid, salty air. I entered my hotel room and turned on some fluorescent lights, which buzzed as if there was a bee trapped inside. The atmosphere was bleak and sterile with a linoleum floor, a small TV, and a coffee maker.

Sitting on the hard, narrow bed, I opened the travel journal I had bought in Sydney and documented my first day of solo travel. The first word that came to mind was "lonely," and I couldn't shake the feeling of emptiness in my gut. *Was it a mistake to embark on this journey alone?* The contrast between this hotel and the suite I'd just left in Brisbane made me doubt my decision to come here. This was so far removed from the previous Christmas, with my sister and all that Victorian splendor and the City of Lights. But I reminded myself that I had chosen adventure, and what's an adventure without some discomfort? I took a few sips of the Bundaberg Ginger Beer I'd collected from the plane and drifted off to sleep.

The next morning, I was up at 6:00 a.m. to take the local bus tour from the town of Seventeen Seventy to Lady Musgrave Island. After nearly two hours of careening through rolling hills with an overcast sky hovering above us and threatening our good time, we arrived at the boat dock. Afraid of getting motion sick, I took a Dramamine and boarded a small craft that sat about twenty passengers. I looked over the side of the boat and could nearly touch the water if I really tried. As we pulled away from shore, huge waves crashed around us, and I found myself rocking back and forth as if I were the ball in a Ping-Pong game. I took another Dramamine just in case and gripped the handles, hoping to stay afloat. The pounding waves continued.

"Are you okay?" our guide asked as she approached me looking concerned. "You look like you're about to get sick." She handed me a brown paper bag.

"I just took some Dramamine, so I should be okay," was all I could muster, although I kept the bag close, just in case.

"Dramamine only works if you take it before we depart. It makes motion sickness worse if you use it while moving," she told me.

I knew I should have read the box. Oh well. It's an adventure, I thought as I hurled into the brown bag too many times to count.

Nearly two hours later, the waters quieted and the clearest blue I had ever seen emerged in the distance. Coral edges poked out from beneath the glass bottom of our boat and offered a peek into the vast ocean world beneath us. The guides handed around snorkeling gear, and I plunged fearlessly into the miraculous waters of the Great Barrier Reef, forgetting the seasickness that had nearly wiped me out hours before. I wiped my goggles a few times to get a better look at the beautiful sea creatures around me. I gently stroked the back of a sea cucumber floating in the water and watched as schools of red, green, and yellow fish swam beside me. My body relaxed in the warm water. I felt transported as I swam to a small island and went ashore, finding myself a quiet corner to reflect in. A year earlier, I wouldn't have believed that I'd travel halfway around the world by myself.

Later that evening, safe on land, I wrapped my arms around my knees and cuddled up in the sand, laughing about getting sick. (The one time I didn't read the manual!) I was so happy that I had persevered to see one of the great wonders of the world. A sense of gratitude and connection seeped into my soul. I was not alone at all. I closed my eyes and said a prayer, asking God to heal the wounds of the past and make me new. To help me find love again and be bold in going after the treasures of my heart. I was teaching myself to tap into the sacred again, and I sought a genuine spiritual connection in the world. As I opened my eyes, the sky transformed into a stunning sight. Shades of pink and purple danced across the horizon.

As the sun sank below the horizon, its warm glow melting into the colorful hues of the sky, a swarm of butterflies suddenly appeared and began to encircle me. With open arms, I ran along the edge of the beach as they danced and fluttered along beside me. It was as if they were responding to my prayers, offering my tattered spirit a symbol of hope and new beginnings. I felt freedom flow within my veins, the type of oasis I'd experienced when pirouetting across the dance floor. Overwhelmed with gratitude, I lifted my head to the sky and thanked God for hearing my prayers and giving me the faith to believe that one day, all my dreams would come true.

Part II
A Passionate Bachata

A playful dance with strong European influences originating in the Dominican Republic. With Spanish-inspired beats, it's a romantic dance done in close partnership.

10

A New York City Dancer at Last

Six months after my magical adventure in Australia, I emerged at Penn Station to the tune of screaming jackhammers, taxi horns, and street vendors jangling my ears with the hustle of Midtown Manhattan. After the sounds, the smell was the next thing to assault my senses. The air was thick with a pungent mix of sewage, steam, and sweat from a city busting at the seams. My senses perked up as my ears were overwhelmed by a mixture of Spanish, French, and broken English from the New York peddlers surrounding me on the street. My eyes danced around, evaluating my new surroundings and sizing up the place to see if I was safe. I wasn't quite sure. I didn't know what to expect when I chose to transplant myself from Southern California to the East Coast to take on a new role at my company. I just knew that I'd felt at home the first time I visited the Big Apple.

I scanned the bustling street, which overflowed with people walking haphazardly but forcefully in all directions. Even though I knew it would mark me as a newbie or tourist, I couldn't help but look up. All 102 floors of the Empire State Building sparkled before me in the fading sunlight, and the building's long tip was lit with changing colors of red, white, and blue in honor of the upcoming Fourth of July holiday. I took this as a personal symbol of freedom, mirroring what I hoped to find in my new adventure.

I took a deep breath and tried, in this moment of reckoning, to conceive that this complicated city was my new home. I exhaled the past, and, along with the acrid scent, inhaled hope for a new future. Suddenly, a stranger pushed past me, jolting me back to reality, so I set a brisk New York pace as I crossed Broadway. I didn't intend to be caught by the city's magic so quickly, but I couldn't help but feel the lure of its energy. I decided to spend some time getting to know the town while I waited for the movers to arrive and unpack my Upper West Side apartment.

After jostling my way through the Midtown rush hour, I finally found myself at the foot of the Empire State Building, eyes up, still caught in the romance and wonder of it all. Then my gaze was drawn down to a black chalkboard sign at the foot of the building with the words "Dance Sport" written on it. Though I didn't yet have the courage to open that door and explore the mysteries behind it, I could see dancers' shadows in the windows above. One of the windows was steamed from the heat that I imagined emanating from each of the dancers as they circled the floor in tight embrace. I grabbed a brochure that was near the chalkboard sign and sat down at the nearby Sbarro to enjoy a slice of pizza. I was ready for the city to feed my stomach and, hopefully, one day my soul.

Two weeks later, I found myself staring out the window of a drab, characterless cubicle, looking down at the ball in Times Square resting motionless in her little cage. I tried hard to fight back tears. The thrill and adrenaline of the cross-country move had quickly worn off, and the reality of my situation was setting in. I had left everyone and everything I knew to start a new job in a new state, with no friends or family to turn to, while I was still healing from my separation a year before. I recognized the irony of starting over again in a new state, like I had done when I moved to California to be with Morey, as the familiar doubts filled my mind. *What was I thinking? How am I going to survive this?*

I felt so alone. Hungry for connection, I invited my sisters to live with me, and they accepted the offer. I was excited to have family nearby once more. Yet even with my sisters in tow, I found myself buried in my thoughts as the excitement of the move dissipated. I was confused and uncertain of how to navigate this new chapter of my life. I had barely started my new job, yet the pressure was already mounting. I was unused to office dynamics after years of working from home. And adapting to city life was not easy. The constant noise, pollution, and lack of space were all challenging. The scream of the subway, taxis, fire trucks, and people walking the streets at all hours of the day and night completely overwhelmed my senses, leaving me short of sleep and not sure how to tune out. I was used to the gentle sound of crashing waves and ocean breezes at my Seal Beach bungalow.

After separating from Morey, Seal Beach had been my sanctuary, a place where I felt calm, peace, and refreshment. I wasn't sure where I would find tranquility in the city until I discovered the rooftop of my apartment building. I had marveled at how lovely it was when the doorman gave me a tour of the building upon my arrival, but I had forgotten about it in the rush of adjusting to my new life. Overlooking the Hudson River, the oasis was hidden on the rooftop among the treetops of apartment buildings, where you could see carefully placed water towers that reminded me of chimney sweepers gliding across rooftops. Our modern building provided lounge chairs with plush cushions, offering a calming oasis and a gorgeous view to the west each evening. I would make my way to the roof with a cocktail in hand, then watch the sunset and sweet sailboats gliding by, mesmerized at the sparkle of the George Washington Bridge as commuters made their way home over the river to New Jersey.

Though I had come with hope and a vision of glamour and

excitement, I was beginning to realize New York, with all its hustle, might not be what my heart needed post-separation. I craved an even deeper avenue of retreat where I could gather my thoughts, gain more courage, and reconnect with myself and my heart. Sitting in my cubicle each day, watching the lights flash in Times Square, I wondered where I would find connection and creative spirit in this unforgiving town. Then, the Dance Sport brochure I'd pinned to my office bulletin board on my first day at work caught my eye.

It took three months to gather the courage to revisit that small chalkboard sign at the foot of the Empire State Building. Walking past it, let alone going upstairs, somehow felt like a daunting prospect. Whenever I thought about it, an uncharacteristic shyness set in, something I thought I had grown out of long ago. But as I settled into my new life, the city's energy began to rub off on me. I found my footing at work and made new friends. Watching Broadway artists carry their instruments on the subway and dancers practice on the platform inspired me to at last try on my own creativity. I thought of the many notebooks and journals I'd kept over the years, capturing my dreams and future plans, and yearned to explore the world as a blank sheet of paper with myself as the author of the story. I signed up for Italian and writing classes and scanned Groupon nightly for the best deals on dance classes, eager to reopen that chapter of my life. When I saw a deal on an unlimited monthly pass at Dance Sport, I knew it was meant to be.

On a brisk early September morning, shortly before my thirty-second birthday, I finally gained the courage to walk through the Dance Sport door, which jingled as I made my way through the narrow hallway to the dingy elevator. With nervous anticipation, I selected the third floor and waited impatiently for the doors to open on the dance studio. It was the first time I had visited a dance studio in over a decade, and I was still nervous to check out the New York dance scene. While I'd never danced in partnership before, I was curious about expanding my repertoire. Besides, the *Dancing with the Stars* show made it look so fun and inviting. What did I have to lose?

When the elevator doors finally opened, I felt as if I'd been transported to a different planet. A mix of Latin and ballroom music filled the air, and through dim lighting, I made out the silhouettes of dancers floating gracefully across a polished wood floor, twirling in perfect harmony. My heart raced with excitement. But my anxious side was tempted to turn around and walk away.

Before my fear could get the better of me, a young woman caught my gaze and smiled deeply as she welcomed me in. "Hi! I'm Amanda. Welcome to Dance Sport. Can I help you?" Despite feeling overwhelmed, I could feel the pull of my old dancing self, the one who loved to perform, edging me toward the dance floor.

"Um, yes. I bought a Groupon for unlimited dances for a month, and I would like to redeem it." I tried to sound confident despite my nerves.

Amanda flashed a welcoming smile as she handed me a brochure and walked me through the different types of classes the studio offered. As I flipped through the pages, my mind raced with possibilities. Salsa, tango, swing, and ballroom—all styles I had admired from afar but hadn't attempted to learn.

My hesitation must have been obvious. Amanda kindly offered, "Why don't you try our Beginner Argentine Tango class? It's a great way to get started, and you'll have a lot of fun." Without giving myself too much time to think, I agreed and followed her to the registration desk. As I filled out the paperwork, I couldn't help but feel a sense of excitement and anticipation for what the night might bring.

The warm smile on Amanda's face put me at ease, and I

found myself more and more engaged with the possibilities. I thanked her, awkwardly grabbed my paperwork, and hurried into the women's locker room. The butterflies in my stomach continued to flutter as I laced up the black chunky-heeled practice shoes I'd bought in haste only a few days before. The creak of the stiff leather against my socks and the unbrushed suede soles slipping on the floor betrayed me—I hadn't had time to break them in. I pulled my long black hair back in a loose ponytail, took a deep breath, and made my way back to the long hallway to find Studio A, the main ballroom.

As I stepped into the bright lights and onto the shiny wood floor, I passed dancers who were laughing, flirting, milling about, and trying on steps. I'd almost forgotten what it was like to be in a dance studio, and I wasn't sure this would be a fit for me. I was convinced I'd made a mistake. The idea of learning new dance styles and performing in front of others excited me, but at the same time, I feared being judged and failing. It was my very first time here, and I wondered if I could bolt for the door unnoticed.

Just as I convinced myself to leave, a tall masculine figure appeared on the dance floor and made his way toward me. Too late. I froze and put on my best guest smile.

"Hi. I'm Paul, the owner of the studio. Welcome to Beginner Argentine Tango." Paul offered his hand, and the gentleness of his smile calmed my nerves.

I can do this.

He signaled for the DJ to start the music, then lined up leaders and followers across from one another. A picture of Al Pacino dancing tango in the movie *Scent of a Woman* hung in the background. Paul had taught Pacino to tango, and I found myself excited to be in the presence of a tango master, teacher to the stars. Paul demonstrated how to raise our arms correctly and encouraged us to simply walk around the dance floor embracing the soul of the music.

I followed Paul in a counterclockwise circle with my right arm raised perpendicularly, my left pulled in across my chest, waiting to be placed on a partner's shoulder. I walked alone and wasn't sure if I was doing this right, but I tried to emulate Paul's conviction as he glided around the room. Much to my surprise, he offered his hand, pulling me into the center to demo the next move.

Paul laced my left arm around his shoulder, my hand gently resting on his back as he pulled me in close. He positioned my head in proper tango form and tightly clasped his fingers around my right hand. Paul's aftershave filled my nostrils as he pulled me into a close embrace, his warmth enveloping me. Though this was one of the first times a man had held me close since the end of my marriage, I felt a sense of security. I closed my eyes and surrendered to the dance, letting Paul guide me across the floor. He walked strongly forward, gliding my feet backwards as his body moved me in the direction of his choosing. I shifted from side to side with his simple forward pressure, as if I were learning a new way to communicate. It was difficult to completely let go of control after the trauma of my marriage, especially with a man, but with each step, I began to feel awakened and alive. Feeling embraced without being smothered was a new experience, and I longed for more.

11

A Bottle of Jameson and a French Balcony

A few weeks later, fueled by my newfound courage on the dance floor, I was ready to start making some of the other dreams I'd imagined in my journals into reality. I convinced my sister Rose to help me celebrate my thirty-second birthday by embarking on a once-in-a-lifetime adventure to the South of France with me. And in that moment of serendipity, a tiny hotel exactly within our budget became available right on the Mediterranean Sea just when we needed it. It seemed magical.

Four hours after leaving Paris, our train pulled into the stop at Hyères, a small town nestled between Marseille and Nice in the middle of the French Riviera. We arrived at what passed for rush hour and were met by a small burst of people making their way home from work.

"Let's walk to the city center," I suggested to my sister, too shy to hail a taxi in French after a decade of not really using my language skills. "It's only two kilometers."

"Yeah, okay." Rose laughed. "But I am not changing shoes with you this time!"

Unlike her larger neighbors, Hyères was barely a small village, and there were no sidewalks or walkways tailored to tourists, only a narrow country road barely wide enough for two cars to pass. Apprehensively, we dragged our suitcases along the dusty roadside for what seemed like hours. The hot sun poured down on my face, and I gently wiped away the sweat droplets accumulating on my forehead.

Are we there yet? I thought, not daring to complain out loud, given our misadventure the last time we walked such a long distance together in France.

A long twenty minutes later, we arrived at the small ramshackle hotel where we'd rented a room. The building stood right by the marina, and paint was peeling from the building's cold white exterior. It was not a luxury resort, but we didn't mind. We were there for an adventure. The man at the front desk begrudgingly murmured, *"Les filles Américaines,"* under his breath as he handed us the keys.

"Don't forget, the reception area is closed until Monday!" he shouted after us, a warning not to bother him on his day of rest. He'd made it clear he was done for the week, done with us, and ready to enjoy his Saturday evening.

"Merci," I replied, then hauled my bags up three flights of linoleum stairs to our room. My sister huffed alongside me, always a trouper.

"We made it," I exclaimed as I threw my bag down and settled into the dusty sofa. *Paradise*, I thought, ignoring the musty smell, run-down kitchenette, and furnishings that clearly had not been updated in decades. All I could think about was the adventure of being in the South of France.

My sister and I quickly made our way to the local market to get some provisions—a big jar of Nutella; a fresh, crusty baguette; soft French cheeses; and a couple of bottles of local Provence rosé wine. When we returned to the apartment, we settled in on the balcony with our refreshments, adding a bottle of Jameson to complete the picture, and marveled at our good fortune in making our way to this little slice of heaven. Although the apartment was sparse, we were in the South of France! We could see the crystal-clear blue waters of the Mediterranean Sea in the distance, and the small fishing village with boats lining the marina made for a stark contrast to New York's jumbled towers and inaccessible waterfront.

As the sun began to set, we closed the balcony door to keep the warmth inside our cozy room as we continued our picnic on the balcony. We toasted with the last of the rosé and giggled in anticipation of the adventures we hoped to have during our week in Provence.

"I'll be right back," Rose said as she moved toward the balcony door.

"Okay," I replied as I took a sip of wine, resting my eyes on the horizon and breathing in the salted air.

"It's stuck," my sister anxiously gasped.

"What?" I replied, not really paying attention as I gazed at the streetlamps sparkling in the distance.

"The door . . . it won't open." Her voice started to tremble.

"What do you mean, it won't open?" I felt my heart race.

"It's locked. It must have been locked from the inside." My sister began to pace nervously across the balcony.

We stared at each other in shock. We were locked out of our third-floor hotel room at 9:00 p.m. on a Saturday evening. As the chill of the Mediterranean air deepened, I thought about the man at the reception desk warning us they would be closed until Monday. My sister frantically pulled out her phone. Although our cell batteries were dying after being uncharged during the long trip, we called our mom, American Express Travel, and anyone else who might be able to help us get back inside, to no avail. After that, we sat on the balcony finishing the last of the Jameson and wondering if we'd be trapped outside all night.

After about thirty minutes of crying and banging and trying to get inside, we spotted a woman walking through the parking lot below. Before I could think of how to respond, my sister started yelling at the top of her lungs.

A Bottle of Jameson and a French Balcony

"Bonjour! Bonjour, mademoiselle! Mademoiselle, help us! Help us." In a near panic, my sister yelled the only French words she could remember. She wasn't afraid to ask for help.

The woman turned and looked up. Her eyes seemed kind, and it was clear her willingness to help might save us.

"Bonsoir," she replied. "*Je ne parle pas Anglais.*" She gently informed us that she didn't speak English, adding another complication to our predicament.

"*Ce n'est pas un problème,*" I replied in broken French, then told her about our predicament. "*S'il vous plaît, la porte est fermée.*" I repeatedly motioned with my hands toward the locked balcony door, and she quickly understood that we were stuck. I was thankful in that moment for my high school and college French studies, and although I wish I had been more fluent, I was able to get us through our situation.

She pointed toward the reception area, noting that she would be right back. For what felt like hours, we waited for the front desk clerk to appear and unlock the door to our balcony. We tried to keep warm by curling our arms around our legs. When he finally came, his face, all curled lips and sneer, conveyed in Gallic fashion his disapproval and annoyance at being called back to help us. He and his wife had made the hour-long drive back from their family dinner when the woman called. His wife glared forcefully at us as she gestured at the lock on the balcony door to remind us how to avoid repeating the dire situation. We bashfully bid adieu to our reluctant rescuers as we returned to the warmth of our hotel room.

"*Nous aimerions vous remercier,*" I fumbled in French to our elegantly dressed savior, Monique, as she headed back into the parking lot. "Can we buy you a drink?"

"*Bien sur,*" she replied—of course. I was glad I could understand a bit of French as we walked to the local café to celebrate our collective victory.

The café had started to fill with Saturday night regulars, and it was difficult to find a place to sit. As we settled into the last free space, I heaved a sigh of relief. I'd been dreaming of adventure, but this wasn't the sort I'd had in mind.

"Let's go to the disco," Monique said in French, jumping up suddenly.

I was not one to say no to a dance party, but after being locked out on the balcony, I wasn't sure it was wise to head out with a near stranger in the dead of night. Yet Rose seemed eager to reclaim the evening with some fun, and I found myself drawn to the idea of an adventure. We gathered our things and made our way through the busy café, climbing into the back of Monique's tiny Peugeot.

The drive felt like a never-ending circle around Hyères with only a rotating light beam as our guide, highlighting the disco's location in the middle of the countryside. *This could end badly*, I thought as I stared out the window from the back seat, all the movies and "stranger danger" commercials of my youth playing in my head. It wasn't like me to get into a car with a near stranger in a foreign country. But it was too late to turn back now. And Monique had helped us. I reassured myself it would be okay.

As we entered the dimly lit disco, the air was full with the universal sound of booming bass and the dazzling pulse of disco lights. My sister and I were immediately swept up in the rhythm, moving as one with the crowd swirling on the dance floor; we danced for what seemed like hours before stepping onto the terrace to catch our breath.

That's when he appeared.

His olive skin glistened in the moonlight and his eyes gleamed with a hint of shyness. As he approached, his lips parted and he spoke in a soft, velvety voice.

"I'm Santos," he said, his eyes never leaving mine.

"*Enchantée*," I said, my heart skipping a beat as I extended my hand to him. As our fingers intertwined, a shiver ran down my spine as if I had found a missing piece of myself.

But before I knew it, my sister grabbed my hand and whisked me back onto the dance floor, leaving this mysterious stranger behind. Lost in the beat, I moved my body to the rhythm, forgetting my brief encounter, my mind and heart consumed by the music.

I didn't remember my short meeting with Santos until the next morning when he appeared at the hotel door bearing freshly picked flowers and an invitation to a traditional French breakfast—rosé wine by the sea.

"How did you find us?" I asked as I stood in the doorway, still disheveled and in my pajamas.

"My friend Monique drove you home last night. Get dressed. Let's get breakfast. My friends are waiting downstairs," he coaxed in broken English with a heavy French accent.

Although I was nervous about joining him, I found myself breaking free of inhibitions on this trip and was intrigued to see what might happen if Rose and I went with Santos and his friends. Plus, the flowers were a thoughtful gesture, and I was ready to say yes to a bit of romance after the previous night's surreal events. I threw on yesterday's clothes, still dance-stained, as I hadn't had a chance to unpack. My sister and I followed Santos and his friends to the nearest café.

The café itself was nothing fancy with simple plastic chairs and a table that had an ashtray in the middle. But the view of the marina all around us was breathtaking. The sun was rising on the horizon, casting a golden reflection onto the sea, which seemed still, like glass. The sailboats in the marina rocked gently back and forth as the cafés along the waterfront began to stir for the day. In the distance, jagged rocks offered a contrast to the clear water, and I could see topless sunbathers basking at a nearby beach.

In both English and broken French, Rose and I engaged in a playful conversation with our new friends, reflecting on the crazy evening that had started with being locked out on our balcony and ended with meeting Santos by chance. We mostly understood each other since everyone but Santos spoke English. The men were from Portugal; they'd come to France to take advantage of the booming economy and support their families back home by working for a construction company. Though Santos was now fluent in both French and Portuguese, his English was less practiced. But his mischievous smile and body language spoke volumes.

Throughout the morning, Santos kept smiling at me in an alluring way, and—with more wine than food in my system—I smiled back, excited at the possibility of the adventures that could arise from our newfound friendship. Tingles electrified my veins as we made plans to spend time together each evening, with a grand celebration set for my birthday at the end of the week. As we drank wine by the sea, the taste of the crisp rosé mingled with the salty breeze. The sound of the waves lapped against the shore and the distant cry of gulls filled the air, adding to our sense of tranquility and freedom. After a day spent savoring the simple pleasures of life, Rose and I finally made our way back to our hotel. We crawled into bed, grateful for the new experiences we'd had and excited to see what the rest of the week would bring.

The next day, my sister and I ventured off on a solo trip to explore some local islands. Stepping off the ferry after a short ride from Hyères to the lush tropical landscape of Porquerolles, the largest of Les Iles d'Or, or the Golden Isles, was like being transported back to the nineteenth century. My sister and I made our way toward the hiking trail, and I quickly realized that I was not properly dressed—I had worn flip-flops instead of tennis shoes by mistake. My lack of proper footwear over the years seemed to be a recurring trend, but I wasn't going to let that mishap stand in the way of having a good time.

It took less than twenty minutes of casual walking along the dusty hiking trail to reach the spectacular vista, and the jagged cliffs surrounding it were uncomfortably close for anyone with a fear of heights. Dust had accumulated between my toes with each step, yet the air was fresh, and I welcomed a deep inhalation to fully experience the beauty of this secluded retreat. When we reached the top of the vista, the view literally took my breath away. I closed my eyes and allowed the majestic views encircling me to etch new beginnings on my heart and soul. The sharp cliffs jutting from the crystal blue water filled my stomach with butterflies for a minute—I was fearful I might take a misstep off the dirt hiking trail. Yet the adventurer in me also started to emerge. I gazed over the horizon, pretending I was armed with binoculars. As the sun started to rise, I felt like an explorer discovering a new world for the first time and the encompassing heat filled my heart with joy. The smell of the air was light and moist, and the hidden lagoons below the cliffs tasted salty and inviting as we made our way toward them.

The winding trail, surrounded by overgrown foliage and what looked like large bonsai trees, emerged throughout our descent. A deserted vineyard led to a swimming lagoon at Plage Notre Dame beach with turquoise water so clear and ice-cold that a brief dip was all we could tolerate. At the beach, women were topless. But with few people yet to discover this oasis, the healing waters of the Mediterranean Sea enticed even timid adventurers. My sister and I hesitantly dove in, embracing the beauty of abandoning our bathing suit tops at the shoreline.

In that moment, an overwhelming feeling of freedom engulfed me, and I felt connected to my authentic self as if she was finally reemerging after so many years in hiding. I had no one to take care of and no worries floating in my head. I was unashamed and free to embrace my womanly shape. I felt like I was finally starting to live my life in color after so many years of living in black and white. I felt beautiful and ready to live life to its fullest. I was ready to start a new year fresh and focused on my own happiness and passions. I could sense more adventure on the horizon.

On the evening of my birthday, Santos and his friends arrived with Portuguese wine and a home-cooked meal, ready to celebrate our last night together. We laughed and talked, and I once again felt warmth and excitement in my heart as Santos and I talked about our uncanny connection, feeling like old friends who could read each other's thoughts despite any language barriers we might encounter. "Soul mates," we kept repeating to each other in English, a word that seemed to translate across languages.

Each time Santos looked me in the eyes, I felt an awakening within me. My spirit somehow felt connected to his, which left me with an afterglow similar to how one feels after meditation or yoga. Tremendous peace filled my being, and a lightness that I hadn't experienced before ran through my veins. As we prepared to say goodbye, Santos kissed me on the cheek. Even though that kiss had been our only intimate connection, the gesture touched me deeply. It was hard to put into words the feeling that emerged from meeting Santos. We had the ability to connect to each other at a profound level without much talk or touch. And something was emerging in my heart that made it difficult to bid him farewell.

In the early morning hours, my sister and I boarded our train to Paris without having slept much the night before. As the train pulled out of the station, tears filled my eyes and a deep sense of loss washed over me. I was afraid I wouldn't be able to hold on to the sweet feeling of vulnerability and connection I'd experienced during our week in the South of France. It was as if someone had unlocked a piece of me that I didn't know existed and I was afraid of losing it. During that memorable week with Rose and Santos, Monique, and their friends, I had come to cherish the simple pleasures of life, for once forming the kind of lifelong friendships and soul connections I so desperately craved. I longed to live in that magical world forever and not let go of the part of myself that had been awakened during our visit. The fear of losing it left me vulnerable since I wanted to hang on to that feeling for good.

12

Rock Star
Wannabe

Within a month of returning home from the trip, I'd nearly
forgotten about that magical week in France and was back
in the balance of work and dance. I was finding a natural rhythm
and was excited that I had a chance to celebrate a career milestone
as I traveled to Florida to attend my Senior Manager promotion event. I'd been unable to attend the celebration for my last
promotion since I was a full-time caregiver stuck at home with
Morey. As the wheels of the plane touched down in Orlando,
tears filled my eyes. Just as I landed, I received a voicemail from
my attorney's office notifying me that our divorce had been final-
ized. This was really it then, a new chapter. I sighed in relief that
the contentious process was now behind me. Though I barely had
time to acknowledge it as I rushed from the airport, I paused to
sit with the news during the ride to the hotel, silently celebrating
the new life that I was living.

On the second-to-last night of my weeklong work trip, our
group visited Universal Studios, and I took advantage of live rock
band karaoke to sing my heart out. Belting out Carrie Under-
wood's "Before He Cheats" in front of my colleagues, I felt like
I was rediscovering an earlier version of myself with each note.
I'm not sure where I found the courage to live out my rock star
fantasy, but I felt my inner passion for performance roar back to

life. The looks of surprise and awe in my coworkers' eyes jolted me as I poured my strength into imitating slashing tires as the chorus progressed. There was something cathartic about being legally free and able to throw my emotions into a song, and I was surprised at just how much passion and soul I had inside, begging to be released. I was hooked. I loved it!

When I got back to New York, I decided to double down on my creative side, so much so that I sometimes got a little side-eye from coworkers as I ran out at the stroke of five, carrying my dance togs with me every night. After my grand karaoke moment, I got bold and signed up for The Singing Experience, a four-week singing workshop that ended with a live cabaret performance in a New York City club. The thought of singing live in front of random strangers still scared me, despite my post-divorce-fueled karaoke—which meant I had to do it. The theme of the workshop was Dream a Little Dream, which felt perfect.

One Wednesday evening, I took the subway from the Upper West Side to Midtown, where my seventy-year-old instructor, a dead ringer for the divine Bette Midler, gathered our group of ten wannabe cabaret performers.

"Can you do scales?" she asked me on the first day.

"Uh, sure," I replied as my palms went cold and clammy.

I hadn't received any formal vocal training since my freshman year of college. I'd been inspired to do something that scared me every day back then, and I'd started with singing classes. I'd practiced a new solo each week and performed it for my classmates, who then critiqued it. It was a vulnerable experience, and I felt myself reliving those shaky preperformance jitters in the small basement practice space as I prepared my cabaret act.

My throat croaked a bit as I attempted to do scales, but with each half step up the scale, my voice started to loosen up.

"Nice job," the instructor offered as I completed my warm-up. *Phew. At least I didn't completely embarrass myself.*

Dancing on My Own Two Feet

It took me a few weekends of scouring the stacks at the Library of Performing Arts to find the perfect song for my cabaret debut. I wanted one that reflected how I felt about the world these days. Among the seemingly infinite green leather-bound scores, Marilyn Monroe's rendition of Jule Styne's "Diamonds Are a Girl's Best Friend" caught my eye. I imagined a sultry performance where I was dripping with diamonds, embracing my flirtatious flair and a sensual side ideally suited to showcasing the sassy moves I was learning in my dance classes. I hummed a few bars, confident I could make up for the mismatch in key with some style and energy. I wanted to make a statement during my first public performance in over a decade, and I thought I knew what I was capable of. With no further consideration, I checked out the sheet music and made a copy to bring to my next cabaret rehearsal.

As I carried my three-ring binder of sheet music around the city after practice, I started to feel like a real New York singer. I joined the ranks of musicians I'd seen on the subway, tuned in to their headphones, practicing their parts under their breath en route to rehearsal or on their way home from a Broadway performance. Okay, so my little cabaret act wasn't Broadway, but it was close!

Four rehearsals later, a year to the day after I moved to the city, it was showtime. Our dress rehearsal was that same day, and I felt sexy in my black satin halter dress, wide faux diamond bracelet cuffs, and dangling clip-on earrings. I had curled my long black hair and added fake eyelashes and bright red lipstick to complete the look. I rolled black fishnet stockings up over my knees and slipped into a pair of two-inch black Latin dance shoes with crisscrossed straps that framed my ankles perfectly.

I stepped onto the tiny cabaret stage that was tucked into the corner of a dimly lit room and handed the pianist my sheet music. I peered into the empty space and started to sing. But with each note, my voice cracked and split. I tried to shimmy my body from side to side to showcase some cha-cha moves, but as I danced, it became harder to breathe and my voice sounded worse. Chagrined and distressed, I finished the chorus as best I could with a splashy flourish and quickly grabbed my music. I tried not to cry as I collapsed backstage in a plastic folding chair watching the other singers perform their parts perfectly.

It'll be okay, I tried to convince myself. *It was just the warm-up. The live performance will be better.*

I took a few photos with my fellow performers backstage, doing my best to summon a smile and some inner strength as we did a final group hug. An hour later, it was my turn to perform for real.

As I peeked out from behind the curtain, I saw my mom and stepdad sitting next to my sisters in the third row. My parents had traveled all the way from Colorado to watch my New York singing debut. Nearly a dozen coworkers and a few new friends from dance class sat close to my family, all eager to show their support. The sold-out crowd of 150 people made me even more nervous, and I felt like throwing up. *What if I croak like I did in rehearsal? How embarrassing would that be?* When my name was called, I swallowed my nerves and strode onto the stage, projecting more confidence than I felt. I took the mic and addressed the audience, ready to let loose as best I could. The heat of the spotlight warmed my face, and the butterflies in my stomach gradually settled. This was my moment, my time to have fun and show the world that I had overcome the challenges of my former life. It was time to make my story known, to no longer hide from the darkness and bring my soul to light.

"I think for a woman, there's no greater time in life than your thirties. You're sweet and sassy—you're coming into your own. And you finally have some words of wisdom to share with the next generation of ladies," I said into the mic. Then, I began sharing my story. "A year ago today, I left my marriage in California to move to this city. My values have changed a little since moving here, and I think I've finally realized what's most important in life."

As I started to sing, my voice quavered and shook a bit, just like in rehearsal, but I didn't let it shake me. I sang each note with conviction and allowed myself to channel Marilyn's sensual stylings. As I launched into each choreographed dance break during the musical interludes, I felt myself come home. It was a challenge to navigate the tiny stage with a baby grand piano taking up much of the space, but I still managed to embody the sensual seductress the music demanded. I forgot my fears and my self-consciousness about my voice; instead, I focused on seducing the audience and moving my body around the stage, making eye contact with each audience member.

For five minutes, I sang and danced my heart out. I felt free. I didn't worry about whether I hit every note precisely. I was owning the challenges of my past and sharing my story with the world. I felt proud of the courage I had found to start over, and I allowed myself to be vulnerable without shame. With dramatic expression and sheer joy, I owned every croaky note as I shimmied and belted out the final chorus, expending all my breath and strength. Striking a final pose, I exhaled into a generous smile and thanked my audience. I bowed excessively as my friends and family cheered in the background.

I did it.

As I stood onstage after my performance, tears threatened to spill over, and I shared another piece of my story with the crowd. "This experience has been a dream come true for me. I used to be a trained ballet dancer. In real life, I'm a CPA. But tonight, I finally ventured beyond financial statements in this city of lights. I haven't performed in a show in thirteen years, and I just came off a very dark chapter in my life."

I took a deep breath and continued, "During that time, I didn't allow my dreams to be limited by my circumstances. I've been a big believer in the power of dreaming, and I used dream journals to envision the life I wanted to live one day. While I did get a little lost during those difficult times, I kept my dreams alive, and today I'm living a life that once seemed like a fantasy. So, I really hope that each of you walk away this evening not only inspired but also with the courage to find a way to make your dreams come true, because they really can. So, thank you so much."

A smile lit up my face as I finished speaking, and I saluted my family and friends, the cheering squad who had supported me through so many difficulties. The sparkle in my eyes was real, and I felt grateful for the chance to perform and share my story to inspire others.

13

The Chronicles of a Dancing Accountant

A few months after the cabaret performance, as summer turned into fall, I waved to my colleagues as I grabbed my dance shoes and shut down my work computer. It was 5:15 p.m. and the Times Square disco ball, which dangled outside the window in my office, was changing colors from hues of yellow to green and blue. Not wanting to be late, I rushed through my shutdown and hustled out onto Forty-Second Street. I was filled with delight by the combination of steam wafting from subway grates and dancing around muddy puddles while making my ten-minute walk to Dance Sport. I had become addicted to this routine as I returned to the studio night after night, arriving home to my apartment around midnight, happily exhausted from dancing.

During each night I spent at the studio, I was learning to feel the movement, listen to my partner's lead, and surrender to the rhythm. It was a new form of communication for me, one that I had yet to fully comprehend, but I felt it was full of possibilities. Each person I danced with spoke a different language through their movement and style—some were quiet and gentle while others were strong and powerful. Some were thoughtful and respectful, others pushy; some hesitant and unsure, others forceful and commanding. I was curious about what I would learn and discover in my nightly adventure that evening.

With each step away from the chaos of Times Square, I felt myself being drawn inward, connecting with the creative parts of me I didn't know existed, or at least hadn't had a chance to connect with in years. Steam from hot dog carts engulfed me as I walked past, reminding me of a movie scene, and I inhaled the pungent aroma. The city that was initially so foreign had become a part of my inner being. Walking the eight blocks, zigzagging between cars, ignoring crosswalk signs, and acting like the true New Yorker I'd become was now my daily jig to loosen my muscles before arriving at the dance studio. After executing a few jeté jumps to move between tourists, I finally arrived at Dance Sport, still in awe each time I walked through the doors, the smell of pizza from Sbarro whetting my palate while the gentle sounds of tango echoed in the air. After months of making this trek five days a week and attending four hours of dance classes and social dance parties each night, I felt more confident when the elevator doors opened. As I walked into my sacred space, I was no longer a stranger. I was starting to belong.

"Hi, Amanda. How are you today?" I smiled at the reception desk as Amanda gave me a quick wave while she checked in a new student who looked as apprehensive and shocked as I had almost a year before. I scanned my key fob, went to the dressing room, and quickly changed into my practice dress and now well-worn ballroom shoes. The black suede leather on the soles had started to fade and I comfortably wiggled my toes as I slipped them on.

My thirty-third birthday was approaching, and I made it a goal to celebrate by taking my ballroom dancing to the next level. Now that my divorce had been official for nearly a year, it was time to leverage my wedding ring to help fund this new adventure. The pawn shop around the corner from the dance studio barely offered me what it was worth, but I told myself that if I could invest in furthering my dance life, it would be okay. I held back tears as I put the $500 in my pocket, ready to offer it to the

113

studio owner the next day as a deposit on a private dance lesson package so I could see what I was made of and work toward becoming a performer again. Getting a few hundred dollars for a ten-year marriage didn't feel like a fair trade, but I tried to focus on the overwhelming sense of freedom that accompanied my release from the ring's bondage and the marriage it represented. Besides, the marriage had never quite fit me. I intended to find growth and peace in this new beginning.

I initially started my private lessons with James, a new instructor from Sweden, with plans to perform in the studio's showcase after our lessons were complete. James's warm smile immediately comforted me the first time we met at the salsa dance party and my spirit felt safe with him—our natural chemistry and a similar sassiness made dance take on a new level of fun. Besides, I was a sucker for a man with an accent. Even though he was shorter than I was, I felt electric when I was in his arms.

"Hi! Ready to start our practice?" I gave James a warm hug and a kiss on the cheek as I entered Studio B, a smaller ballroom tucked in the back of the building that would be all ours for the next hour.

"Always," James replied with a sly grin as he started the music.

I could feel the beat of the cha-cha music as he made his way to me, already starting to move his hips while offering me his hand, inviting me to join him in a warm-up. I felt my heart racing, my palms sweating, and my legs shaking from nerves since this was my first private lesson. And yet, despite my obvious anxiety, I felt so alive. James smiled at me, calming the flutter in my tummy as he grabbed my hand. An electric current circulated between us, and I smiled back, ready to start. I felt a little light-headed, I imagined like the experience of falling in love, even though I was still unfamiliar with that.

"Are you ready to start?" James asked in his gentle Swedish accent.

"So ready," I replied, wanting to melt into his arms.

The Chronicles of a Dancing Accountant

When James brought me into a gentle hold, I felt safe in his arms. For the first time in my life, I was dancing with a man who had no desire for me, or for women in general, which created an immediate sense of freedom in my spirit. I didn't worry about whether he would hit on me or things would get too close for comfort. Instead, I was excited to play, let loose, unleash my sensuality in a safe way, and fully embrace the power of the song we were embodying in our lesson, "What Makes You Beautiful." I hadn't always felt beautiful—my intimate experiences with Morey had mostly been stained with trauma. What beauty remained within me, I wasn't sure of yet. But I knew that each time I closed the nightly social dance parties at Dance Sport, I felt more and more like the confident nineteen-year-old I once was—the person who, only a few months before marrying Morey, had performed a sensual solo from *Chicago*. Expressing myself creatively through dance allowed me to reconnect to an earlier version of myself, one that was less damaged and pure. I wanted to reclaim her spirit and improve it by incorporating the wisdom I'd learned from each experience I had endured along the way. I wanted redemption for the battle scars lining my heart. I hoped dance could help repair and restore the beauty and undo any damage that I'd done by ignoring my own needs and desires for so long.

As James stretched into cha-cha walks to the beat of the music, his torso puffed like a peacock on the prowl, and my body loosened from the cage it had lived in for so long. With each step forward and back, following James's lead, I felt lighter, more in tune with the gentle spirit and loving heart that had led me to say yes to Morey for as long as I did. I started to imagine that my easygoing nature and desire to please weren't tragic traits but superpowers that I had over-calibrated and allowed to be used against me. With each song lyric, I let go of my remaining shreds of shyness, insecurity, and inhibition and held my head high, moving my body in unison with James. His spirit, as gentle as it was, met me exactly where I needed to be and felt like everything I had craved for over a decade due to the harshness of my relationship with Morey. My inner essence lit up with each sly flirt and flick of my dance heels on the wooden floor and was transported throughout my body and soul as I expressed my creativity. I glanced at myself in the mirror. The smile on my face was genuine and there was a sparkle in my eye that I hadn't seen in my adult life. Both dance and James were helping me realize just how beautiful I was.

It was a Thursday night, and I was still flying high from my private dance lessons with James the week before. I was excited to continue our work together while also exploring different dance styles with other instructors. The freedom unlocking in my spirit was unlike anything I had previously experienced, and I was excited to test the waters with additional dance instructors. My newest instructor, Sven, was also from Scandinavia, but his personality couldn't have been more different from James's. With James, dancing was all about the music—finding the perfect song that would inspire me to embody emotion. I was hoping for the same magical connection as I made my way to the other side of the dance studio, where Sven was waiting for me to begin our practice of the paso doble.

"Hi, Sven." I waved from the corner as I put on my dance shoes to prepare. "I found a great modern song that I thought would be really interesting to try paso doble," I offered as I made my way to the entertainment center where he stood.

"Hmmm. Well, paso doble is a very traditional dance. I'm not sure it works with contemporary music." Sven's tone was matter-of-fact, and he made his way to me without any accompanying music.

"I see," I replied, feeling defeated.

My gut cringed at his critique, which felt incredibly personal given the value I was placing on finding myself through dance. The pit in my stomach that had often accompanied critical moments with Morey flashed through my body as if this small criticism was making me second-guess my opinions or thoughts once again. I wondered if I should push harder with Sven, but I didn't want to offend him, and he was so precise in his movements that I decided to let it go.

"Okay. Let's start by practicing our frame when we're together in ballroom hold." He placed my left arm around him and laced his fingertips into my right hand as he motioned for me to lift my chest and look over my left shoulder.

My body felt rigid and tight as we walked together in silence, making strong back-and-forth motions with our heads and arms, like the bull and his master. As we danced, I felt the part of me that had been blossoming slowly shrink. *Two steps forward, one step back*, I thought as we continued in a counterclockwise motion around the dance floor.

"Let's do it again until it's perfect," Sven said. We practiced each move repeatedly until he was satisfied it was pristine. Only then did we move on to learn a new move—all without any music accompanying us. My heart sank with each silent move. I remembered my teenage days in the ballet studio, taking time to practice each move over and over until it was perfect, which eventually burned me out.

When the lesson was finished, I gave Sven a side hug as I made my way back to the dressing room and fought back tears. *Why didn't I speak up for myself and tell Sven how important it was for me to dance to music that inspires me?* It was starting to dawn on me that creating perfect moves wasn't the point (at least not for me; it was clearly very important to Sven). Rather, I craved expressing the emotion that came from tapping into my own inner depths and spirit by connecting through music.

I wanted to cancel my remaining private lessons with Sven because I was haunted by flashbacks of constantly ignoring my needs during my time with Morey, and I didn't like that I now faced a similar feeling of neglect. I still hadn't perfected the art of asking for what I wanted—and then sticking to it. The obedient girl in me made it hard to pick up the phone to cancel. I'd also have to see him around the studio, and I didn't want things to be awkward. *Maybe it was just the first lesson. Maybe it'll get better*, I told myself. I ultimately decided it was at least worth finishing what I started.

Every week, Sven and I met in a silent studio to perfect each paso doble march, hand styling, walk, bow, dip, frame, and hold. I felt like I was in an endurance battle to bring attention to every minute detail until it was etched into my body and part of the fabric of my soul. The dance required persistence that brought me back to the rigid feeling of juggling the balls of work and life with Morey, and I wondered if this was a test of what I was really made of.

Meanwhile, my work off the dance floor had picked up steam and I was spending every other night working till midnight to make it through our reporting deadlines. Work felt hard, and my lessons with Sven felt harder. At least I could still look forward to hearing music during my lessons with James, which gave me a sense of freedom and fun. But the combination was making me sick. My body was tired and my soul felt defeated. I tried my best to advance in my career during the day and live out my dream of being a semiprofessional dancer at night. I ran back and forth between dance and work commitments, barely sleeping. I felt the familiar pointe dancer in me reemerge, ever so gracefully balancing the demands of work and life. I wondered if I would always have to navigate this challenge. *Why am I pushing myself to the limit in all aspects of my life? Will I find a way to express my needs and not succumb to my partner's advances without question?* It was an urgent question. I didn't want to repeat the mistakes of my twenties in this new phase of life.

14

Around the World in Three Dances

The variegated color of an East Coast fall had shifted into the gray of winter. Trees were bare and leaves crunched underfoot, ready to enjoy a season of hibernation. Between work, dance, and spending time with new friends, I was feeling bolder in my ability to try new experiences, though balancing all the areas of my life was still a constant struggle. I even started to date a bit, finding that dance was a fruitful source of potential suitors. Yet no one compared to the wonderful soul connection I had found with Santos during my brief sojourn in France. I couldn't get him out of my mind. We'd casually stayed in touch on Facebook over the last year, but there was nothing serious given that we lived several thousand miles apart.

Despite all my commitments and obligations, I decided to distract myself with another international grand adventure. I made it my goal to make all my vacations the following spring and summer dance-themed, fueled by a growing passion for creative expression. My strength and confidence continued to grow as I learned new dances, and I wanted to keep pushing myself to see what else I could discover. I decided to travel to the dance capitals of the world that I had yet to explore and match them with my newly learned dance styles. I planned to waltz in Vienna, samba in Rio, and tango in Argentina. I had never been to these cities before. I was excited to experience them through the lens of dance and deepen my connection to this art form.

My first stop was Vienna, where I planned to dance the Viennese waltz. Instead of staying in a touristy area, as I had on previous trips to London and Paris, I opted for a small traditional hotel on the outskirts of town so I could experience Austria like a local. On my first full day in Vienna, I took the bus to Tanzschule Elmayer, one of the city's most famous waltz training centers. The small dance studio had been in operation since the early 1900s, and I had signed up in advance for a sixty-minute private lesson with one of the instructors.

As I stepped off the bus and onto the narrow cobblestone street, which was lined with boutiques and inviting little restaurants, my heart began to race. I was less afraid of venturing off into a new city than I had been during my first time in Europe, but since this was my first time dancing in a foreign country, I wasn't sure what to expect. I kept careful note of the street signs as I made my way to Bräunerstraße13 where I saw the distinct yellow "Tanzschule Elmayer" sign hanging above the entrance.

Checking the time, I realized I was a few minutes early and took a deep breath as I opened the door, hoping to make a quiet entrance. The bell jingled behind me, and a young woman greeted me in German from behind the reception desk.

"*Guten Morgen*," she said.

"Good morning," I replied, still a bit shy to use the little bit of German I had learned on the train. "I'm here for my private lesson." I handed her a printed confirmation of my appointment.

"Of course! Welcome to our studio. You can get ready in the dressing room behind you, and Hans will be with you shortly," she replied in perfect English.

As I made my way to the changing room, I could see a group of fresh-faced teenagers, clearly self-conscious, filing into the front ballroom for etiquette and dance classes. Each girl wore long white gloves and a flowing dress while the boys sported suits, ties, and impeccably shiny shoes and belts. They nervously joined hands to practice traditional waltz and folk dances in anticipation of the balls that would be the culmination of their program. Not wanting to add to their self-consciousness, I averted my gaze and quickly changed into a long dance skirt and my ballroom practice shoes. After waiting in the reception area for a few minutes, a young man, barely twenty, approached me.

"*Guten Morgen.* I am Hans, your dance instructor," he said with a strong Austrian accent.

"*Guten Morgen.* I'm Jenn. Nice to meet you," I replied as Hans offered me his hand and led me past the group of aspiring young dancers to a smaller private ballroom.

"What would you like to work on during our time together?" Hans asked.

"I would love to spend some time practicing traditional Viennese waltz and then explore some other dance styles," I offered, a smile forming across my face as I expressed my desires without any hedging or apology, something I was getting more accustomed to.

With that small bit of instruction, Hans took over. He pulled an old-fashioned LP out of its sleeve and delicately placed it on the record player. I felt the 3/4 beat in my head and began to internalize that special lilt of Viennese as he increased the volume. *One, two, three; one, two, three.*

Hans approached me and guided my arms into a proper ballroom frame. As the music started, he took my hand and led me to the center of the room. We started with the basic steps, gliding across the floor in a graceful spin. I could feel the music in my bones, and Hans's guidance was so gentle and precise that I was rapidly lost in the dance. I couldn't help but smile as we spun around the room, absorbed in the beauty of the moment.

As we danced, I kept my posture strong and turned my head

to the left as I let my mind relax. Relinquishing control and following Hans's movements taught me more than just dance; it showed me how to trust myself and have confidence in my own desires. As the music's tempo increased, we whirled around the dance floor, my skirt twirling beneath me with each turn. We repeatedly circled the perimeter of the floor, and I felt that wonderful, graceful buzz of the Viennese waltz. I took a moment to reflect on how far I had come and how proud I was of myself for embarking on this solo dance journey. I thought about what it meant to be in that studio at that stage of my life as we twirled and twirled.

The steps gradually grew more complex, and my mind began to flit, worried I would make a wrong step and stop our momentum. I tried to focus on letting my body simply respond to Hans's lead. I felt like a fairy-tale princess in my practice shoes and plain rehearsal skirt, gracefully navigating the floor with Hans. Despite my nerves, I was living my dream of dancing the Viennese waltz in Vienna.

I would have pinched myself to make sure it was real, but I was doing my best to maintain a proper frame and stay in sync with Hans as he continued to twirl me around the dance floor. As the music slowed and finally came to a stop, I couldn't help but grin with joy for taking this chance and giving myself such a memorable experience. After a few rounds of the waltz, Hans suggested we switch to another dance style.

"Now that we have practiced the waltz, why don't we see your Latin moves? Can you do a cha-cha?" he asked with a sly smile, as if offering a challenge.

Can I do a cha-cha? Ha! He has no idea! After nearly a year of working with James on my Latin steps, cha-cha had become my sweet spot and I was always down for a little hip action.

"Of course, I can," I replied with confidence as Hans walked to the music station to change the tune. The upbeat music filled the room, and I whispered the rhythm to myself, feeling more at ease in my own skin, ready to show Hans my moves.

He approached me with a renewed sense of energy, clearly more at home with the cha-cha than the waltz. He pulled me closer and we moved in unison as we cycled our way through some basic moves. As we danced, our bodies swayed and our hips moved in rhythm. Hans broke into freestyle moves and I followed his lead, matching his energy and adding my own flair.

Hans guided me through the steps, his hand firm and confident as we moved together as one, and I found myself delighted by the joy and flirtatiousness of the dance. As we flirted and chased each other across the dance floor, I felt myself connecting more deeply with my inner self, the one who had been reawakened by my dancing in New York. I became the version of myself who was confident, sensual, and fearless. I took his invitation and followed him front and back multiple times, moving my hips and crossing my feet as I made my way closer to him, swinging my hair and turning away with a flirty grin that tempted him to pursue me to the other side of the dance floor. As I unleashed more of my attitude, I started to shed years of self-doubt and insecurity, and my inner grace further emerged. The playful glint in my eye and the sway of my hips made me feel alive and beautiful again. This was not the woman I'd expected to meet when I walked into the room, but I was thrilled to have rediscovered her.

At the same time, Hans transformed in front of me. He seemed genuinely taken aback at my American-style cha-cha, and I could see the flush rise in his cheeks, changing his reserved demeanor. Our dance was bolder and sexier than the structured, by-the-book International Ballroom form he was clearly used to. It felt like I'd introduced him to a new experience, and as the music ended, we both giggled with delight like teenagers on a first date. He'd helped unlock a flirtatious side of me I'd long forgotten. And I? Well, I like to imagine I left him with some interesting ideas about American dance, and perhaps American women.

As our hour came to an end, I was reluctant to leave. Dancing with Hans had been an unforgettable experience, and I knew I would carry the memories of that morning with me for a long time. As our lesson finished, I thanked him and planted a kiss on his cheek to say goodbye. With a deep bow and a heartfelt danke schoen, I made my way back to the dressing room already planning my next visit to the Tanzschule Elmayer. As I walked out the door, I looked back at the sign above the entrance understanding that somehow, I was leaving with a stronger sense of self than I'd had when I first arrived. I took an inner snapshot to remind myself of this unexpected gift. I began to feel I was really regaining my power.

15

Falling
for His Charm

With renewed confidence and craving some romance, I reached out to Santos. Now that I was in Austria, we were almost in the same time zone for the first time in a year and a half. After a few short-lived relationships with men I didn't really connect with off the dance floor, I was yearning for something deeper. That flirtatious dance with Hans had left me daydreaming about my magical week with Santos in the South of France. I thought of our nights at the café and our long walks by the marina watching the sunset. When I got back to the hotel after my dance lesson, I sent Santos a short and sweet text. I had butterflies in my stomach and the warmth in my soul reignited as I awaited his response. When he quickly replied, I began to feel as if I was in a dream state and the rest of the world had faded away.

I spent the rest of the week in a daze, waltzing from text to text as video chats with Santos rekindled our connection. I couldn't wait to retreat to my small hotel each night so I could hear his voice and see his face after taking in the Austrian sights. We would fall asleep talking via FaceTime, with our phones gently tucked into our respective pillows. Our uncanny connection deepened with each remote encounter, and Santos suggested I come to see him in France while I was in Europe. We'd decided we wanted to see if our friendship could be something more. As

Santos's English skills improved, we shared our mutual wish not to succumb to superficiality, which we both agreed seemed to monopolize modern relationships. That's when I decided to change my plans and visit France to see what might be possible with Santos.

He believed that what mattered in life was spiritual and pure. He also believed in a higher power, and we shared a desire to live life fully and with abandon. Together we embraced a carpe diem approach to life and vowed to make the most of it. This philosophy greatly appealed to me, especially after the nightmare of living as a prisoner in my home for so much of my married life in California. On the last night of my Vienna dance adventure, and before we had spent another day together in France, Santos officially asked me to be his girlfriend. I eagerly anticipated my arrival the next day. I was sure that this was what being in love felt like.

As my plane touched down in Nice the next morning, I took a deep breath. I felt nervous to see Santos after spending a year and a half apart. Despite our declaration the night before, our friendship had not yet turned romantic, and I wasn't quite sure what to expect. What if the chemistry I'd felt over a year ago and through the Internet wasn't real? Physical intimacy outside of marriage was still new to me, and I wanted to take things slowly. Our initial time together had been limited, and though we felt such a strong connection, the language barrier still made more subtle communication difficult. But I was willing to put my heart on the line to see what was possible, hoping our soul connection would last. I headed out of the airport into the warm sunshine and was greeted by a familiar face.

"Monique! *C'est bien de te voir!*" I hugged my balcony savior, thrilled and surprised to be reunited after so long apart. She'd offered to pick me up at the airport when she learned I was coming. Even though we barely spoke the same language, the warmth of her hug settled any qualms I'd had about the trip. It felt like that moment in a movie when best friends reconnect after decades (I could practically hear the music swell), and I was starting to feel more at ease. If we could connect so easily, surely the same would happen with Santos.

I threw my bag in the back of Monique's familiar Peugeot and we started the ninety-minute drive to Santos's apartment outside Hyères.

"I can't believe you are here. Are you excited to see Santos?" Monique offered in halting English. Clearly, she'd been practicing for my arrival.

"*Mais oui,*" I responded. I really was excited. I continued in the best French I could muster, asking how things were going with her boyfriend and how her family was. But mostly, I focused on the rolling hills and sweeping ocean views in the distance as I eagerly awaited the reunion with my love.

As we pulled up outside Santos's apartment, I took another deep breath and emerged from the car, my eyes straining at the bright sun and clear blue sky. I looked around, expecting to see my love, but he hadn't arrived home from work yet. I grabbed my bag from Monique's car and stood in anticipation, my hands once again clammy from nerves.

As I lifted my sunglasses, I caught sight of Santos out of the corner of my eye, making his way hesitantly toward me, his hands overflowing with a bouquet of vibrant red roses. His aviators glinted in the sunlight and his black leather jacket and faded jeans added to his charming European flair. I saw his sly, familiar smile, and before I had a chance to fully take him in, he leaned in for a sweet little kiss on the lips. We melted into a warm and long embrace. Despite the nerves and shyness that lingered after our long separation, I couldn't deny the longing my soul felt for this man. Monique smiled as she waved goodbye.

"Welcome, my love," Santos greeted me. He grabbed my bag and my hand, then led me the short distance to his apartment door. As we stepped inside, I could feel the butterflies fluttering again, this time with a combination of anticipation and trepidation. I couldn't believe I was really here after being away from him for so long. The memory of our happenstance meeting after my sister and I were locked out of our French apartment flooded into my mind. I wondered, *Am I really taking this step?*

I took another deep breath as Santos welcomed me to his home, which he had thoughtfully prepared for my arrival. He placed the roses in a vase at the center of the dining table, which was lined with lace and set with wine glasses and a bottle of the local rosé. Santos had made space in his small bedroom for me to unpack my things, and he'd artfully arranged a set of personal toiletries in the bathroom so I could freshen up.

We made our way to the balcony to toast the beginning of this next chapter.

"Soul mates," Santos said in English, raising his glass.

"*Saúde*," I offered in return, a salute in his native Portuguese, which I had been practicing back home in New York.

"I can't believe you are here, my love. My heart is happy." Santos leaned in and gave me another kiss on the lips. His lips tasted of sweet wine and cigarettes, and my stomach fluttered with butterflies. This felt right.

We delighted in being back together, reminiscing about how we met at the disco and how shy we'd been during our first week together. We marveled at our mutual feeling that we were soul mates. But mostly, we made new memories—officially toasting our relationship together and embracing the vulnerability of falling in love. After an evening of wine and conversation, the sun began to fade over the horizon, casting shades of pink, orange, and purple across the sky and reflecting off the ocean waves glistening in the distance. Santos took my hand and gently led me to his bedroom, where we nervously embraced in an intimate way for the first time. I hadn't been sure if there would be physical chemistry between us as we had only kissed on the cheek before our reunion. I also hadn't been sure I was ready to go all the way on our first night together. But being together in person made me abandon my preconceived ideas and feelings about how I should be. I felt safe in his arms and was willing to trust him with my heart.

The next morning, I woke to the sunrise peeking through the barely covered window. I looked out to see the magical hues of a sunrise awakening the small town. Santos was no longer beside me, and I took a moment to take it all in and bask in the glow of our connection. It was as if a part of me that had been dormant for decades finally awakened. Tears welled up and my stomach leapt with joy. Though I was still getting used to being together and felt out of sorts in a new country, I was also strangely at peace. *This must be what it feels like to be in love*, I thought once again. *This feels right.*

Santos unlocked a part of me that I didn't even know existed. Whenever I was in his arms, my responsible side, which had been my constant companion since childhood, disappeared. I found myself daydreaming and imagining a life of pleasure and simplicity instead of constantly planning, achieving, and engaging in an endless quest to take care of others' needs, which had been my lot for most of my life. I was drawn to the idea of enjoying a glass of wine in the morning with my love and letting the day unfold without trying to control everything or worrying about what might happen. My childhood and my marriage had both been consumed by tending to others, along with feeling obligated and pressured to perform, and I was amazed at the mere idea that there could be a different way to live.

As if on cue, Santos knocked quietly on the door and entered the room bearing a tray filled with bread, coffee, and sweet treats for breakfast in bed. He gave me a sweet kiss as he handed me an espresso.

"Bonjour, my love," he smiled.

"*Bom dia*," I replied in Portuguese, sprinkling a third language into our conversation.

"Let's go explore the town today," he suggested, excited to show me around.

After we finished breakfast and got ready for the day, Santos took my hand and led me to the beach. He showed me a Buddhist temple he found inspiring because it reminded him to "embrace Zen" in a world of chaos. He also talked about his resistance to conforming to traditional social norms and his desire to live a life of pleasure and adventure. I'd never dated someone with this approach to life, and I was both intrigued and a bit shocked. He didn't feel uncomfortable breaking the rules—he had even lost his driver's license and didn't worry about driving without one. He also wasn't afraid to be late if he needed time to have coffee or smoke a cigarette. In fact, "late" wasn't really a part of his vocabulary. He approached life with an ease that I found fascinating—and foreign. Imagining a life of simple pleasures and challenging the status quo to live on one's own terms felt refreshing to rule-abiding, structured me, and Santos definitely played by his own rules. I wondered, *Could I do the same*?

We stopped at a beachside café for a glass of wine as we continued getting to know each other. Santos dreamed of becoming an architect one day and building his own home in the countryside, complete with a vineyard where he could cultivate his own wine and live a simple life. His family had been vintners in the past and he was longing to make *le rêve* (the dream) a reality.

Santos's outside-the-box thinking inspired me, and I wanted to join in. But going against the grain had always been a struggle for me. Santos listened as I explained the challenges I had faced in my marriage, and he understood when I told him I was still healing and needed to take things slowly. He was gentle and loving, and his eyes greeted me in a way that made me feel truly beautiful.

Each time I started to analyze what our relationship would look like and how we could manage a long-distance romance, Santos encouraged me to *laisses tomber*, let it be. I loved this simple, empowering phrase, yet I found it difficult to fully embrace. I wanted to have a life plan in which everything was figured out. I wanted to know where we would end up in our relationship and how we could logistically make a long-distance relationship work. I liked order and knowing what to expect, but that didn't seem to be on Santos's radar. He was okay taking things one day at a time.

As day turned to evening, we got dressed up for a night on the town, and I let myself try to relax and go with the flow. Santos drove us a short distance to another restaurant with a Buddha statue in front. The restaurant was simply named The Buddha Bar, and inside, the dark venue looked like a typical bar filled with locals ready to enjoy their Friday evening. We sat at the last open table, which was tucked in a back corner, and ordered a drink.

"I have a surprise for you," Santos said excitedly.

"I love surprises," I replied, even though I really didn't, then gave him a kiss while I waited in anticipation.

"Look over there." Santos pointed to the front of the bar, where a three-piece band was setting up on a makeshift stage.

The band started to warm up, the rich sound of guitars and drums commingling as a woman started singing in Spanish. I recognized the music's familiar beat almost immediately. It was a smooth bachata, an intimate dance that I loved from my classes back home. The music tempted me, its sensual beat already loosening my hips and enticing me to come out and play. Santos grabbed my hand, inviting me to the dance floor.

I was surprised and touched. Santos was shy, and not a dancer, but he knew how important dance was to me. He also knew that bachata had become one of my favorite Latin dances. He held me close as we moved side to side—*one-two-three-tap*. Our hips entangled in the rhythm of the bachata basic, the one move Santos had learned before my arrival. My eyes flirted with him, grateful for the sweetness of this unexpected gift. A sly smile was loose on my lips and my hair was free-flowing, my long tresses caressing the sweat forming on the back of my neck from the growing heat on the dance floor. As we moved to the rhythm, it felt like the rest of the bar disappeared, as if we were the only ones in the room.

The simplicity of the dance allowed me to focus on the energy of our partnership and decide if I wanted to learn more or move on. Even though I could tell Santos was nervous, I felt an electric pulse between us. Suddenly, I felt so comfortable in his arms. As the song finished, Santos beamed with joy, delighted in the success of the surprise he'd set for me, and I felt the sweetness of our connection.

On the last night of our weekend together, we spent the night in a hotel on the coast of Nice, close to the airport, so we could relish every last moment of our time together. We walked hand in hand along the coastline, where beachside bars sparkled as the sun dipped past the horizon. Santos pulled me close as the temperature dropped, wrapping his gray scarf around me. I inhaled the mix of cologne, cigarettes, and his leather jacket as he whispered repeatedly in my ear, "Soul mates."

I squeezed Santos's hand as we walked through the streets. I imagined our future together in America or in France. I knew I'd have to wait for it, but at that moment, I was sure it would be worth it. "Let's do our best to make this work," I pleaded. "We can visit each other and stay connected. I don't want to lose you." I was speaking as much to myself as I was to him, not wanting to release his hand or his love from my heart.

"Yes, my love. We will be together forever," he replied, kissing me softly on the forehead and drawing me in close. I hoped it, willed it, begged it to be true.

16

A Purple Tango Shoe and a Ninety-Year-Old Argentinian

Four months after I began dating Santos, during the week leading up to my thirty-fourth birthday, I was struggling to shake off a nasty cold. Santos and I had snuck in a quick trip to Paris for a pre-birthday celebration. We were doing our best to stay true to our promise to fly back and forth to see each other even though the in-between times were getting harder to handle. Jet-setting from country to country and dance to dance was taking a toll on my immune system, yet I didn't want to let a sore throat stand in the way of wrapping up my year of dance adventures. As I said goodbye to Santos in Paris, I was excited about my upcoming trip with my two work besties, Ellen and Jocelyn, who were joining me in Rio for a few days to celebrate before we headed to Buenos Aires to dance with the tango maestros.

The day before my birthday, I flew alone to Rio de Janeiro's Galeão International Airport and took a cab to Leblon, an upscale part of the city. As the cab driver wove his way through the narrow streets, I couldn't help but feel nervous. The outskirts surrounding the airport were incredibly poor, with favelas lining the hillsides. People were selling snacks and water in the middle of the road, but the cab driver accelerated past them, his eyes never leaving the road. Santos had warned me to be careful, and I could see why. Yet I was excited to explore a new part of the world even as my nervousness lingered. As my cab approached the city, I could also see why Rio captures people's hearts. Lagoons, large mountainsides, and beaches appeared from all angles. My usually impeccable navigation skills were out of whack, and I couldn't quite figure out which way was north or south. The cab driver dropped me off at the Marina Palace Hotel and I took a deep breath of sea air, my nerves calming down a bit.

I checked into a modest one-bedroom suite on the ninth floor of the hotel, which boasted a prime location right on the waterfront. It was only a short drive from the renowned beaches of Copacabana and Ipanema. Although the hotel was basic, it was adequate for my needs, and I was grateful to have a place to rest my head after a long day of travel. As the first of my group to arrive, I was happy to have some time to myself. I threw my bag on the floor and crawled onto the makeshift cot in the living room, taking a moment to reflect on the fact that I was visiting yet another continent. It was hard to believe that just four years earlier, I had only begun to imagine this different life for myself. Yet here I was, living it to the fullest. Later in the evening, my friends would join me to dance and celebrate my birthday, but for now, I was content to be alone with my thoughts. *I made it.*

Brazil marked the twentieth country I had ever visited and the seventeenth I had explored since my marriage ended. It was astounding to see how much my life had changed. I had mustered the strength and courage to embark on solo travels and adventures with my friends and family members, making my way across borders and soaking up diverse cultures. But it wasn't just about seeing the sights and ticking countries and continents off my bucket list. I was enriching my cultural experience by incorporating dance into my travel adventure. Dance had become a window into my soul. Ever since reigniting the flame of that passion at Dance Sport in New York, I was determined to keep it burning. And I had opened my heart to falling in love.

As I rested at the hotel, my cold started to subside, and I knew I needed to hydrate after the long flight to Rio. Afraid to drink the local water, I ventured out of the hotel and onto a bustling Leblon street. As night fell, the city came alive. Light posts beamed with welcome and warmth illuminated my path to a small grocer on the corner nearby. I purchased two large water bottles and paid the cashier a few Brazilian reais, exchanging a smile with her as I settled my purchase.

As I emerged into the muggy twilight, I felt a million miles away from the woman I used to be, the scared woman who had spent her days riddled with guilt and had worried for years about leaving an unhealthy marriage. That woman was no more. I was finally free, and I was thousands of miles away from my past life. I realized I was finally finding my way back to my true self. And what better way to celebrate than to dance!

When I was searching for an authentic Brazilian samba experience before the trip, I came across the Rio Samba Dancer online. The company offered a package that included a group samba dance lesson at a local dance studio followed by a guided visit to the Rio Scenarium, one of the city's most famous dance clubs. Located in the Lapa area of Rio, the club featured live samba bands almost every night and drew thousands of dancers.

After a quick group lesson at a nearby dance studio, Ellen, Jocelyn, and I stepped onto the Rio Scenarium dance floor. The windows of the classic European-style building were open, letting in a humid breeze. The space was filled with people moving to the music, their passion and vibrations contagious, the energy in the room electrifying. The owner of Rio Samba Dancer pulled me to the center of the dance floor and we danced together, our hips moving in harmony. We held each other close as we moved from side to side, our hips shaking in sync and smiles filling our faces. As the music reached its climax, my dance partner spun me into an elegant pose like a professional peacock on the prowl, and I felt invigorated and powerful. When the dance ended, I gave my new partner a hug and made my way to the bar to order a passion fruit caipirinha. The experience was unforgettable, and it left me yearning to find that passion in my own life, not just on the dance floor.

A few days after our samba adventure, Ellen and I traveled to Argentina to explore the tango scene in Buenos Aires, also known as the tango capital of the world. I knew that Ellen wasn't a tango dancer so I would likely be visiting the tango salons alone, but that brought out the adventurer in me. I felt confident, strong, and bold knowing I had prepared for this moment with my practice back home, and also through my European travels.

Feeling adventurous one afternoon, I stepped into a small shop that sold tango shoes. The door creaked as I opened it, betraying my presence. As I tiptoed alone into the tiny dusty space and my eyes adjusted to the light, I could just make out the shelves of men's and women's shoes on either side and a simple bench in the middle. There were boxes scattered everywhere. The store smelled faintly of wet leather and a milonga tune played on the radio.

"*Hola! Bienvenido,*" a middle-aged woman called out. Noticing my hesitation, she continued in English, "Can I help you?"

"I'm looking for some tango shoes," I mustered as I gently stroked the leather strap of a pair that was on display. I looked around. "These are beautiful," I exclaimed, admiring a pair of animal-print shoes dyed a deep shade of purple, my favorite color.

The shop owner quickly brought out several sizes for me to try on. I thanked her as I found the perfect fit and buckled the strap.

"You tango?" An older man appeared from behind a stack of shoeboxes at the back of the store, apparently surprised to find an American shopping for tango shoes in this obscure part of town.

"Yes. I learned in New York City," I answered as I stood to admire my feet in the tango stilettos.

"Then we must dance," he insisted. "*Música, música*," he called, and the saleslady turned up the radio.

Before I knew it, he had me in a firm tango embrace. I found myself stepping back in classic *ochos* steps, pivoting my feet as well as I could across the worn carpeted floor. Wearing my new tango stilettos, I towered over the stocky elderly gentleman, who nonetheless had a flawless ability to navigate the carpeted floor as we danced, helping us both to avoid the empty shoeboxes scattered across the floor. The dance was far from perfect, but we both laughed and enjoyed the moment.

"You're ready," he said with a broad smile, and I felt I had passed an audition I didn't know I'd signed up for.

"I hope to see you later at the Confitería Ideal Milonga—it's just down the street," he said. The bell on the door jingled as the elderly gentleman made his way out to the bustling Buenos Aires street, leaving behind a whiff of pomade.

"I'll take these," I said to the salesclerk, handing her my credit card. She wrapped up the purple shoes with care.

I felt like Dorothy, ready to take on the tango world with new ruby slippers—except mine were purple tango shoes. As I left the shop, I couldn't help but feel a mix of anticipation and nervousness for what the night might bring.

Later that day, when I made my way to the Confitería Ideal Milonga, I passed my new favorite tango shoe shop and a host of local businesses. The excitement of finally experiencing my favorite dance form in its birthplace coursed through me. The legendary tango salon, one of the oldest afternoon salons in Buenos Aires, had been a gathering place for devoted tango dancers for over one hundred years. With its imported European crystal chandeliers, dark oak paneling, Italian stained-glass windows, and marble stairs, the salon exuded a sense of old-school elegance and sophistication. It was as if I had stepped back in time to a golden era. I had read about this famous tango salon in the Buenos Aires guidebooks, and I couldn't wait to experience the dance in action at this iconic venue.

As I prepared, I was struck once again by the intimacy of the dance. When danced properly, tango requires partners to be as close as possible, creating a deeply magnetic connection. The dance calls for a combination of spontaneity and deep listening, with partners attuned to both the music and each other's body language to pick up on signals while also offering a clear structure that includes specific customs for how dance invitations are made and accepted. Tango holds an important cultural significance in Argentina, and while it was originally embraced by working-class European immigrants, it has now been integrated into the highest society. As I stepped toward the dance floor, I took a moment to embrace the long dance lineage I was about to experience.

Full of anticipation, I hurried to the side of the dance hall for my official dance lesson. There I joined three others, all clearly beginners. The instructor was an arrogant young man, barely thirty, who taught us the proper way to perform a tango embrace. I waited my turn as we slowly walked in circles around some folding chairs that marked the border of our makeshift dance floor. I had been dancing tango with professional tango maestros for several years now, and I quickly found myself getting bored rehashing the basics with this youngster. After breaking in my sweet purple tango shoes by performing a few *molientes* and *gauchos*, then taking a short water break, I yearned for a turn on the main dance floor. I grabbed my things and quietly exited stage right, making my way past the elegant tables and velvet chairs that lined the perimeter of the grand ballroom. I took a seat at a small table, marveling at the exquisite architectural details that silently told the story of this famed *milonga*. I sat quietly as elderly dancers floated in; most appeared to be in their eighties and nineties, making me by far the youngest in the room.

Feeling out of my element, I basked in the opportunity to be here even though I was alone. I closed my eyes and remembered my first experience with the tango. After so many years with Morey, I'd needed a safe way to rekindle my ability to be gently caressed and cared for, to touch and be held. Tango met that need and restored my soul. When I first began, I didn't realize that dancing the tango would be the beginning of a journey to find inner peace and strength.

As the music changed during the *cortina* (a short break after a dance set) and dancers made their way off the floor to seek new partners, an elderly gentleman approached me. He was formally dressed in a black tailored three-piece suit that barely covered his waist. His hair was slick and combed back, a deep gray that reminded me of my grandfather.

"*Bailar?*" he whispered, offering his hand and inviting me to the dance floor.

I glanced over my shoulder, fully anticipating that I'd misunderstood and someone else was on the receiving end of this invitation. I hadn't danced yet, so I was surprised at being invited to the dance floor before anyone could see that I knew what I was doing. Instead, I saw the gentleman I'd danced with at the shoe shop. He gave me a thumbs-up as if he himself had prepared my new partner to ask me to dance after our audition in the shoe shop. I smiled as I accepted my elegant new partner's outstretched hand. I gently lifted my arms and wrapped them around my partner as we took hold in a tango embrace. I closed my eyes and let the music guide me as I took my new shoes out for a spin.

A Purple Tango Shoe and a Ninety-Year-Old Argentinian

The wooden floor creaked beneath me as I merged into my partner's steady frame and allowed my feet to slowly move backwards with each of his gentle nudges. My shoulders relaxed and followed his lead as the sound and spirit of the music engulfed me. Sweat dribbled down my forehead, discreetly staining my cotton dress, but I didn't take notice. My mind and body were transported to another universe, as if we were floating in the clouds without a care in the world.

Dancing the Argentine tango in Buenos Aires that afternoon did more to heal my inner spirit than therapy ever had. In that moment, it was not about choreography or technique; rather, it was about self-expression in its purest form as I felt the orchestra's gentle pull and listened only to my partner's heartbeat. The dance did not need to be perfect. I wasn't trying to collect gold stars or achieve an award, but I felt our inner spirits talking to each other. I released the pressure of perfection and allowed myself to lean into the power of connection, a dance that can only be truly experienced with closed eyes and an open heart.

The somatic trauma I'd experienced during my marriage to Morey—I'd often conceded to his wishes during intimacy even if I didn't want to—was etched deep within my body. With each gentle embrace from my dance partner, I felt the tethers of that trauma loosen. As my partner stepped back, gently asking me to follow with the forward motion of his body, I felt free to listen. I didn't follow simply because it was being demanded. Instead, I willingly chose to join the partnership. There was something about being in such close partnership with a man who felt safe to my spirit (which, by now, was almost whole again) that allowed me to relax and be on that dance floor. The world around me was hazy, my partner and I the only ones in focus. As the music of the three-song *tanda* ended, the gentleman, whose name I did not know but whose spirit I had learned on the dance floor, graciously escorted me back to my seat.

"*Muy bien! Perfecto,*" he whispered as he let me go.

I slumped into my chair, trying to catch my breath. I was completely at home and at peace, and I took only a moment before looking around for my next partner.

17

Reconnected
in Lisbon

Three months after tangoing in Argentina, I breathed a sigh of relief as my plane touched down in Lisbon following a seven-hour journey from Florida. I had spent Christmas in Cape Canaveral with my family in a blend of laughter and agony. My job rotation in New York was nearly up, and I wanted to grab the chance at a prestigious fellowship in DC to open up new career possibilities. I spent more time than I would've liked glued to my computer over the holiday break, revising my application rather than enjoying time with my family. Leaving New York was hard to imagine. After just three years, I'd fallen in love with the city and the version of myself I'd discovered there, but I was ready for a fresh adventure. And this time, I knew I would have a community of friends as long as my life included dancing.

I had planned a trip to visit Santos in Portugal for New Year's but was thinking about canceling—I wasn't sure it was the responsible thing to do, given my application deadlines. But I remembered Santos's Zen philosophy, which had been rubbing off on me more and more. I was tired of sacrificing joy for my responsibilities. It was another new year. *"Laisses tomber,"* I said as I pushed the "send" button to submit my draft application to my supervisor.

I landed in Portugal before sunrise, and the airport was eerily quiet; it was empty and dark except for a few maintenance and security folks and the rare gate agent waiting for an overnight flight to arrive. Santos had texted me before I left to say he would take the train and meet me at the airport. As I emerged from customs, my eyes darted in all directions, searching for my love. When I didn't see him, my anxiety immediately kicked in. *Is he okay? Did he make it? What do I do now?* Just as my thoughts started to get the best of me, I turned a corner to see Santos curled up in a ball on an airport bench, his leather jacket crumpled in the shape of a pillow. Disheveled as he was, he looked sweetly sexy in a gray V-neck T-shirt that hugged his body, along with his signature tattered jeans. As I approached him, he awoke and offered a sweet smile hidden behind a yawn.

"Did you spend the night in the airport?" I asked, hoping the answer was no.

"Yes, my love. I didn't want to be late. Don't worry—I'm okay." He slicked a hand through his mop of sleep-tousled salt-and-pepper hair.

Santos had struggled to be on time in the past, and as part of his *laisses tomber* attitude, time wasn't as critical to him as it was to me. He was clearly trying to please me by spending the night on an airport bench rather than risk arriving late. I was just thankful we were together once again.

"Let's take a coffee," Santos suggested as he took hold of my hand and luggage and led me toward the only open café in the deserted airport.

We had officially been together for seven months, mostly long-distance, and I was still fascinated by Santos's laid-back attitude and penchant for frequent coffee breaks. But as someone who didn't drink coffee and who was accustomed to a New York state of mind, I often felt impatient and eager to get to our destination while waiting during these breaks. After sipping a leisurely double espresso and smoking a cigarette, Santos appeared more refreshed. We headed to the train platform and boarded a 7:00 a.m. train to the Algarve, Portugal's southern region.

During the four-hour journey, both Santos and I were lost in our own thoughts. I hadn't seen him since he visited me in New York over Thanksgiving and we traveled to DC to explore whether it would be a suitable place for us to begin our lives together, assuming everything went as planned with my fellowship. I hoped Santos would be willing to give America a chance even though we had originally talked about building a life together on a vineyard in the South of France. Our time in DC was a mixed experience. Santos indulged me by taking a private bachata class. There was chemistry between us when he held me close even though I could feel his hands trembling from nerves. It was his first formal dance lesson, and he wanted so much to please me. Those memories were very sweet.

However, when we visited a few colleges to explore architecture programs in the district, things became a little uncomfortable between us. Santos, a grown man in his forties, had been constructing schools, malls, apartment buildings, and private homes for decades. Even though he was self-taught and lacked a formal college degree or certification, he was a man of experience. I couldn't stop picturing him laughing in disappointment when he'd seen the model buildings that he would construct out of toothpicks if he went back to school. "Toothpicks? I build these buildings for real. This is a joke!" he muttered under his breath when we toured the University of Maryland campus.

I could sympathize with Santos's reaction, and I would have been let down, too, if I were in his shoes. But I knew it would be difficult for him to find a job in the US right away unless we were married, and it felt too soon to consider that level of commitment. If he studied in the United States, we could be together. When we parted ways after our East Coast adventures, we'd already planned a trip to Portugal, his home country. It would be a good test to see what our relationship was made of.

Santos was not great at maintaining communication while we were apart. Though we had started our relationship with blazing texts, his responses became slower over time, and my heart ached for days when I didn't hear from him. I wondered, *Has he given up on us? Is he seeing other women? Am I bothering him?* I felt so vulnerable, and I constantly craved connection, admittedly because it was the key to opening a part of myself that I had only just discovered; I wanted to hang on to the feeling that our connection aroused in me. I found myself becoming obsessed in the silent void, waiting for his rare responses, repeatedly checking my phone and debating whether I should text him again. *Did he get my text? Why isn't he responding?* I felt like a junkie waiting for her next hit to keep the magic alive. Every response, even if it was only a few words, fueled me in my search for more. I felt our connection shifting, and I wanted to hold on.

Our silent train ride south finally came to a stop as we approached the station near Porches. I looked out the window to see blue and white tiles lining the platform. We made our way to the taxi line, and after fifteen nearly silent minutes, we arrived at our destination. It felt odd to spend so much time together in silence. I knew Santos had a tough time opening up and expressing himself, particularly in English. Still, despite not feeling completely at ease, I was excited to explore a new country and celebrate New Year's with my love.

We found our way to our hotel. It faced the sea, and the sun shone in the center of the sky. It was a brisk sixty degrees, which felt refreshing for a late December day. I opened the porch door and was instantly awestruck by my surroundings. Jagged rocky cliffs the color of sand emerged from the sea line, creating a stark contrast with the ice-cold blue waters that bellowed beneath them. Each cliff housed secret dwellings where water flowed in and out with each breath of the moon. In the distance, a small white chapel at the end of a cliff caught my eye, its steeple glowing in the sunlight and inviting us to take a closer look. I grabbed Santos by the arm and we made our way to the narrow walkway, feeling like we were on top of the world. Seagulls gathered around us, taking time to stop and pose for pictures. I felt the same magic I'd experienced on the beach in Australia when butterflies surrounded me at sunset, and my heart no longer felt alone.

A few minutes later, I entered the tiny white chapel's quiet sanctuary. I dropped a few euros into a small coin box and lit a candle, closing my eyes to say a gentle prayer. I thanked God for helping me find the courage to leave my marriage and start again. Being with Santos and witnessing his unapologetic belief in the spiritual realm had helped me reconnect with my own beliefs. I felt gratitude for experiencing the beauty of the majestic sunset that was beginning at the end of the rock pier, and I said a thankful prayer to God for helping me finally unlock a part of my soul that had been buried for nearly a decade. I ducked my head as I emerged from the chapel and gave Santos a sweet smile and a kiss on the cheek.

"I feel blessed," I shared, curling into his arms to watch the sun dance down the horizon in a spectacular display of magical colors. It was nice to experience this beauty with someone I loved. After the sun set and chilly air enveloped us, Santos and I made our way back toward our hotel.

"Let's take a coffee," Santos cajoled as he pulled me into a small coffee shop that also served as the local bar. We played darts and laughed, and I tried my best to enjoy the moment.

Toward the end of a quiet week together, I picked up the keys to a two-door rental Peugeot, slid into the driver's seat, and buckled my seat belt, ready for a one-night adventure. I apprehensively put my hand on the gearshift, trying to calm my nerves. Although it had been a decade since I'd driven a manual transmission, I encouraged myself: *You can do this.*

I took a deep breath and smiled at Santos, who was patiently waiting for me to start the engine. He looked sexy in his leather jacket and crooked smile. Santos's driver's license had expired months before and he, with his laissez-faire philosophy, hadn't gotten around to renewing it. Though he'd previously driven us around without one, I didn't feel comfortable this time since the rental contract was in my name. I turned on the ignition, put the car into gear, and nervously pulled out of the dealership next to our hotel complex in the Algarve.

The car made fitful progress, seemingly stuck in second gear. I tried to remember when I'd learned to drive a stick, way back in Colorado with my father teaching me. As we finally got up to speed, we passed small white churches with their steeples glistening in the sun and homes with terra-cotta roofs. Children played soccer in the streets, and the cobblestone sidewalks accentuated the slower pace embraced by our Portuguese neighbors. I accelerated and shifted gears as we made our way onto the expressway and headed east toward Spain. Santos put his hand on mine and, with a smile, whispered, "Sexy," clearly impressed and turned on by my ability to master the unfamiliar stick shift. Still, I couldn't fully suppress my annoyance at being the only legal driver.

I mindfully watched the road as the landscape changed to rural villages and open spaces interspersed with suspension bridges that seemed to appear out of nowhere. In my rearview mirror, the sun was gently descending toward the horizon and the landscape was mostly uninspiring and dry from the winter weather. Santos and I once again stayed mostly quiet during the two-hour drive, something we were both getting used to. My thoughts were occupied by the unfamiliar terrain and manual transmission, the revisions I needed to make to my fellowship application, and the late start to our journey. I wasn't sure we would make it to Seville in time to see a flamenco show, my only real wish for this mini adventure. Santos had made our hotel arrangements, and I kept hinting at my desire to see the dance show, but he brushed me off each time I mentioned it.

As the sun began to set behind us and the sky turned a golden hue, we pulled off the highway into the city of Seville. I wasn't quite sure what to expect, but I was immediately disappointed. Cars whizzed by at breakneck speed, the narrow streets were less charming than those of the Algarve, and my blood pressure rose as I struggled to keep the car safely on the road. There were fountains and cafés on every corner, yet it was much more metropolitan than I was expecting. I had hoped for the charm of a rural Spanish village to bring out my cozy side as Santos and I walked hand in hand through town. Instead, I felt transported from the paradise of the Algarve to the hustle and bustle of Paris or Buenos Aires—wonderful cities, but not what I had been hoping for. My anxiety rose with each narrow street until we finally entered the hotel parking garage.

After checking in, we made a beeline for the rooftop to catch the sunset's last fleeting amber glow. Hues of pink, orange, and bronze laced the hotel's outer edges and light glistened off the windows, highlighting Santos's olive complexion. He pulled me in for a deep kiss.

"We made it, my love," he whispered, seemingly without a care in the world. "Let's go explore." Santos grabbed my hand and we tumbled onto the busy street as the day turned to night.

As we turned the corner, I ran to the first fountain I saw and struck a classic flamenco pose, capturing the city's passionate energy. Santos snapped a picture and we settled into a nearby restaurant for some tapas, sangria, and paella. I tried not to check the time with the arrival of each small bite. The flamenco show would be starting soon, and I was nervous we wouldn't make it.

I glanced at the souvenir shop across the street, where small figurines of flamenco dancers taunted me with the disappointment I'd feel if we did not get there soon.

"Let's try and see a show," I said one more time, but Santos pretended not to hear.

I tried to ignore the pain in my gut, reminding me of the traumatic silent treatment I used to receive from Morey. As we walked back to the hotel, my annoyance continued to simmer, and I gave up on seeing a flamenco show that night. We made the return trip to the hotel in silence, and as the clock approached midnight, I knew we would not make my flamenco dreams come true. When we arrived back at our small but cozy hotel room, I immediately took a seat at the small desk and turned on my computer to revise my fellowship application. As I worked, I realized my frustration with Santos went beyond missing the show. Despite our efforts to make a long-distance relationship work, I knew deep down that he wasn't the right partner for me. It was too difficult for Santos to open up, and I didn't feel completely comfortable being myself around him. Despite his caring nature, he couldn't be there for me in the way that I needed.

I tried to ignore the knots in my stomach and the tears that threatened to fall as I worked on my application. I pushed aside my questions about why Santos hadn't made more of an effort to ensure we made it to the show and instead continued ruminating on the fact that I wasn't in the type of relationship I wanted to have. It wasn't about the missed dance show or lack of driver's license. Deep down, I knew that no matter how hard I tried to convince myself, we weren't a match. I craved emotional connection and depth, yet all I seemed to get was the abyss of a silent void. As I turned off my computer and climbed into bed with Santos, I knew, despite my sadness, that I would soon say goodbye to him for the last time.

After that night in Spain, our remaining time in Portugal

was—perhaps unsurprisingly—far from what I had hoped for. My fellowship application consumed more time than I had anticipated, and Santos was increasingly irritated each time I broke out my computer.

"Don't you understand how important this is to me?" I would ask, but it fell on deaf ears.

On New Year's Eve, Santos started getting stir-crazy and was ready to do something special. "Let's make fettuccine," he suggested, gathering ingredients from the local market and setting up shop in the hotel room's tiny makeshift kitchen.

I appreciated the thoughtful gesture and thought back to our first week together when he brought me a homemade meal to celebrate my birthday. I nodded in agreement and returned to my computer to edit my application for the umpteenth time. That evening, over glasses of wine and plates of creamy fettuccine, we watched the sunset fade into night from the comfort of our private balcony. After dinner, Santos offered a New Year's toast.

"May all your dreams come true," he said, raising his glass to mine. I avoided his gaze, instead looking at my computer, which hummed in the background.

"Cheers," I replied, returning to my laptop shortly after dinner was over.

I wasn't sure if my compulsive need to work on my application was driven by my desire to achieve success or if it was an excuse to distract myself from my intuition that our relationship wasn't clicking. As the clock approached midnight, I didn't have time to dwell on the thought. I powered off my computer and joined Santos on the balcony to welcome the new year. We waited in anticipation for the year to turn the page. As it did, the coast erupted with the sound of champagne bottles popping in celebration all around us. Fireworks in shades of silver and gold lit up the sky, and Santos leaned in for a kiss that blended with the salty air. We lingered for a moment in the hopes and possibilities of a new beginning, but the distance between us had grown, and not even a magical evening in paradise could keep us from saying good-bye. As the sound of fireworks faded into the distance, beneath a sky filled with stars, Santos and I made our way back to bed in silence. We had to catch an early train to Lisbon in the morning, and I had a long flight to New York the following day.

"Good night, my love," Santos whispered.

Au revoir, I thought, but I couldn't bring myself to say it out loud.

The train ride to Lisbon was quiet, as expected, but I was irritated instead of calm. During our taxi ride to the station, Santos confided that he had run out of cash. *Here we go again*, I thought. *Someone else that I need to take care of.* I handed Santos a few hundred euros so he could make the train ride home. Normally, this wouldn't have been a big deal—things happen, and couples support each other in times of need. But there were too many little things. Being with Santos had unlocked a part of me that I wanted to keep open and free, but it came at a cost. He wasn't as responsible as I wished; he couldn't drive or fully support himself in traveling outside the country. But the bigger issue was that he didn't meet my emotional needs for connection and communication, especially when we were apart.

"What's wrong, my love?" Santos asked, sensing my agitation.

"I'm just thinking that this is our last night together and I'm sad to see you go," I equivocated. I still hadn't quite figured out how to be completely honest about my feelings.

Santos offered a hug to appease me, without any words of comfort.

Once we arrived in Lisbon, we dropped our things at the Sheraton near the airport and walked hand in hand through the dark streets for a final dinner together. We discovered a tiny café,

El Chamois, where the waiter placed a generous appetizer platter in front of us featuring fresh cheese, prosciutto, kalamata olives, and a baguette.

"Vino?" the waiter asked.

Both of us nodded without hesitation.

"My love, I know this week didn't go as planned. I know you wanted to see a flamenco show in Seville, but I knew we wouldn't have enough time, so I tried to distract you," Santos explained.

"Why didn't you just communicate that to me instead of hiding your feelings? I know I've been preoccupied with my application, but this fellowship is really important to me, and I needed to focus," I replied.

"I know, my love." Santos put another olive in his mouth, staring pensively into the distance.

Our food arrived shortly after, the delicious pork chops and roasted potatoes stopping our conversation as we enjoyed our meal. When we'd devoured the last morsel, the waiter returned.

"Café?"

"*Sim, dois*," I replied, holding two fingers in the air, ready to enjoy a final espresso with Santos.

After we settled the bill, we walked quietly back to the hotel, not quite ready to face each other in our room. We sat on plush velvet chairs in the lobby and ordered glasses of wine as James Blunt's "You're Beautiful" played on repeat in the background.

"I love you," Santos began, looking into the distance. "But I can't give you what you need," he continued in broken English. "And so, I have to let you go." Tears rolled down his cheeks.

Tears streamed down my cheeks, too. I was in disbelief as the song lyrics replayed in my head. I didn't argue. I knew he was right, and I appreciated his honesty. But even though I'd been thinking the same thing, I didn't want to believe it. I didn't know what to say, but I knew I didn't need to spend a decade with Santos to discover we weren't a good match. My instincts were speaking clearly, and I was finally ready to listen. But that didn't mean it hurt my heart any less to hear it.

Laisses tomber, I finally told myself. It was time to let go.

The next morning, I wore my sunglasses as I boarded the plane and walked down the aisle to my seat. My eyes were swollen from crying, and I knew my heartbreak was only just beginning. Looking out the window, I recalled the train platform where we said our goodbyes. My heart ached in disbelief.

We had embraced earlier that day, in the center of Lisbon, both grateful for our time together and saddened by the abrupt end to our romance. As Santos boarded his train to France, I waved a gentle goodbye and turned around. A part of me remained on that platform, and I walked through the station in a daze, heading to the airport, trying to move on.

18

A Butterfly Emerges in the City

When I returned to New York, my heart was disheveled. I cried my way through the finishing touches of my fellowship application and threw myself into the best therapy I had found to date: dance. I knew the only way through the pain was forward, and I could only hope that some learning would emerge on the other side, making this heartache worth it.

Hoping for a distraction that would bring me back into my body and help me to forget the longing I felt for Santos, I poured my broken heart into practicing a hustle with a new instructor, Francisco. He fully embodied masculinity with his chiseled muscles and height that exceeded mine even when I wore strappy ballroom heels (finally!). I appreciated his lighthearted personality and the playful smile that lit up when he danced.

I was scheduled to perform the dance on Valentine's Day as part of a dance show at a new studio, and my practice schedule was the shortest I'd had to date. I was nervous, but I knew I would lose the North Star that guided me back to myself if I didn't turn to dance while healing from the last few months. During our six-week practice, I joined Francisco three nights a week at a new studio in the center of the Times Square chaos. Work was picking up, and though the walk from my office to the new studio was shorter than my commute to Dance Sport, it felt just as fraught as

I lugged my office bag through a maze of tourists with cameras dangling from their necks as they meandered through the stream of flashing lights, honking horns, and half-naked characters scattered around Times Square looking for their next photographic mark to pay the bills. Each time I arrived in the small studio on Seventh Avenue and West Forty-Fourth Street, I took a deep breath, wiped the sweat off my forehead, and gathered myself before taking the stairs up one flight to greet Francisco in the large ballroom we shared with several other dance instructors and students.

"Hi, Francisco. So great to see you," I said as I gave him a kiss on the cheek and rushed behind a small curtain to slip out of my ballet flats and into fiery red practice shoes. I secretly hoped the fire in my feet would work its way into the rest of my body and remind me that I would find love again, true love. But there was not much time to think as Francisco made his way toward me with playful merengue steps, swaying side to side. I smiled as I felt some warmth in response and my heart fluttered a bit.

"Okay, sweetie, let's put the finishing touches on this sassy dance. Today, let's perfect our lifts, dips, and connection. I want the audience to burn with desire when they see us come together with our bodies in tune with the song." Francisco was already circling his hips in a figure eight, and I felt our natural chemistry enhancing my passion for dance.

I laughed a little, blowing him a playful kiss as he made his way to the music station and waited for his turn at the console to play our song, "Give Me Everything." The sensual song choice was not an accident. I had chosen it when Santos and I were together since it was one of his favorite American tunes, and I decided to keep it as a remembrance dance of our chapter together. I figured I might as well pull off the Band-Aid of heartache and channel my sexiness to bring the dance to life—hopefully while processing my loss and reconnecting my soul with my body. It turned out

Francisco appreciated the out-of-the-box song choice as much as I did and was all in to make it sexy and fun.

As the music filled the air, Francisco seduced his way back to me. I let my body melt into both the music and my partner's muscular arms. Francisco looked me straight in the eyes as he gently guided me across the floor, in and out, with a disco flair in a hustle perfectly crafted to contemporary music. At first, we started slowly as we played our seductive parts, working to give each other everything we could, as the song lyrics demanded.

Francisco gently lifted me in his arms and swung me around, embracing me as a lover might. My heart fluttered as I longed for the feeling that I'd felt with Santos. I also felt a quick flash of yearning for the life I'd imagined—one without modern conveniences, embracing French vineyards overlooking the Mediterranean and rosé on a Sunday morning in the arms of my man. I gently wiped away the tears that fell freely as Francisco caressed the small of my back, leading me out into a hustle strut so I could flaunt my inner diva on the floor. A gentle smile made its way to my lips, and I held my head high, catching the eye of the woman in the mirror before me, a woman who had found love and loss again but who was also strong enough to channel her pain into this dance. That woman was a long way from the shy girl who had redeemed a dance Groupon three years before.

The beat of the music quickened, and the fire between Francisco and me continued to heat up as we made our way around the dance floor, in and out of each other's arms. For me, the dance was an expression of the spirit of my relationship with Santos. As the music met its peak, Francisco lifted me into a swan hold, spinning me around like a child on a carousel, and I felt myself reconnect and heal. The uncanny soul connection I'd often felt in Santos's presence suffused my dancing body as if my veins were filled with warm blood for the first time in a very long time.

Dancing on My Own Two Feet

In that moment, as I danced with Francisco, I realized that my ability to connect with my inner wisdom didn't depend on a person, place, or experience. Not Santos, not a vineyard in the South of France, not my travels, not my job, not even my dance partners. It was within *me*. I started to see that Santos had served a special purpose in my life—he'd been a beacon to light my own internal fire. It was now up to me to keep that flame alive.

As Francisco continued to glide with his arms around mine, directing me in each move, I began to understand that, soul mates or not, Santos and I weren't meant to be together. I couldn't change him, but I had done my best to appreciate our precious time together for its own sake. As Francisco and I continued to circle the floor, executing a series of intricate moves and holding our connection, our bodies communicating through subtle cues and signals, I felt the profound connection and heartbreak of my time with Santos begin to shift, lifting my spirit as I danced. I was really starting to live life again, with all its quick turns, sudden shifts, and spins. That was a tremendous transformation in itself. I realized that I would be able to leverage inspiration and power—on or off the floor—without being dependent on someone else. I was more than a dancer preparing for her next performance; I was a transformed woman who could appreciate the experience of a relationship that ended in heartbreak and find closure in knowing there was still much good to be embraced.

As the music faded and Francisco lovingly carried me off the imaginary stage to signal the end of our performance, I realized that each experience, both on and off the dance floor, was preparing me for a greater ability to love again and connect with myself. I smiled as I thought about how so many little choices had made such a big difference in my life. Who could have known that a bottle of Jameson and being locked out on a French balcony with my sister would incite such a profound transformation?

Part III
A Soulful Tango

An intimate dance, originating in Argentina, that taps into the depths of one's soul. It's best danced in close partnership with a safe and trusting partner.

19

Founders Club

Nearly six months had passed since that dance with Francisco, and I'd obtained the accounting fellowship in Washington, DC, after working so hard on my application while I was with Santos in Portugal. It was my first day on the job. I was excited to serve as a regulator at a large federal agency, and I looked forward to stretching my brain in a new way, seeing a different side of the accounting profession, and meeting new people.

I took my oath of office alongside a dozen or so fresh-faced fellows. "Do you promise to protect investors and uphold your commitment to the public interest?"

Raising my right hand, I replied without hesitation, "I do."

I took a deep breath. It felt thrilling to commit to a greater purpose in the accounting profession. I was proud of my accomplishments, and I was especially excited to take this step, but it was also hard to start over in a new city *again*. Saying goodbye to NYC the week before had not been easy. But I was ready for a new adventure, and I felt much stronger than I had when I first landed on the East Coast, unsure of how to make my own way.

I'd found it easy to make decisions about where I wanted to live, how I spent my money, and which apartment felt like home—a stark contrast to how I'd experienced my early days alone after my divorce. Travel, dance, and love now fueled me, and the scars of my prior life were at last beginning to fade. I felt young once again, though another milestone birthday—my thirty-fifth—was just around the corner. It couldn't have been more different from my thirtieth.

To launch my new life, I leased a one-bedroom apartment in upscale Bethesda, Maryland, within walking distance of the metro, just across the DC border. I'd sold my car to my brother when I moved to New York, and I was determined to stay car-free as long as possible since I enjoyed being a city girl. Naturally, the most important criterion in choosing my new lodging was proximity to ballroom dance studios. I knew I'd have a home base and a community as long as I was involved with dance, and I'd done my research. I'd let Morey talk me out of this fundamental part of myself when I moved to California, but I wasn't going to make that same mistake again. I planted myself just one block from two ballroom dance studios, pulled my dance shoes out of my travel bag, and told myself I was ready to begin.

I quickly signed up for an introductory private lesson at each local dance studio to get a flavor of the instructors, but it was several months before I mustered up the courage to attend the weekly social dance parties. It had become second nature to go dancing alone in New York. There, I'd regularly seen a crew of dancers who had gone through the system at the same time as me. But I had yet to find my footing in this new environment, and the shyness of my early years reemerged. I wondered if my confidence and courage had been partially fueled by New York's inspiration and energy. DC's governmental atmosphere felt different. Here, I had a sense of purpose and was inspired to change the world through my day job, but my creative passion required a lot more work.

After I began to settle, I realized that choosing a suburban spot on the city's outskirts had some downsides, and the dance studios might not be enough to overcome my feelings of isolation.

And even in the city, DC wasn't New York; it wasn't as easy to feel like I was part of the buzz—I would have to work for it. Despite wanting to connect, I felt profound loneliness in my new home. Without friends (and without my sisters living with me, as they had in New York), I didn't feel brave enough to go to the social dance parties at first.

I often found myself thinking, *Maybe I should just move back to Colorado to be with my family. Is this life in DC really what I want?* On my loneliest days, I was tempted to reconnect with Santos even though I knew our romance was over. The attraction of building a life in the South of France had never quite left me. I cycled through these thoughts nearly every day for the first few months in my new job. But I had learned that it was normal to feel disconnected for at least six months when adjusting to a new place. *I must be patient*, I told myself whenever the familiar anxiety reared its head.

Meanwhile, I took comfort in a few familiar treasures I had brought with me to my new city. I still had the blue dishes and the matching blue couch that had comforted me through two moves, reminding me of my refuge on the beach after I left my marriage. These talismans signaled how far I had come. I filled the bookcase I had put together while planning my escape in California with new books about dance and travel, and I found a place in a cozy corner of my new bedroom for the little white writing desk where I had spent so many nights journaling my feelings and imagining the future I'd make for myself. It was now dimpled and chipped from travel and use. I also hung the sheer purple curtains that had once shielded me in my beach refuge when I was hiding from Morey. I then added a brand-new dining room table, imagining the possibility of hosting guests or sharing meals with a new boyfriend. I began to feel like I had created a home.

The constant noise and vibrating energy that had so jangled my nerves during my early days in New York had become a familiar and comforting presence, and I wasn't used to the eerie silence that enveloped me when I was home alone in my new apartment. My government job was also very different from the public accounting work I had done for so long. While I enjoyed the stability of a more classic nine-to-five job, I struggled with the decreased flexibility and formal structure as well as learning a whole new form of office politics and adjusting to new rules and a new boss. I missed being able to work from home or work while traveling. I wasn't sure I felt comfortable being so grounded.

But I loved the friends I was beginning to make, ever so gradually, at my new job. Each day, a growing group of us (mostly new hires) would take a break from our desktop computers and government offices and wander over to the vaulted halls at nearby Union Station. We'd wander the food court and fill our bellies with Bojangles, Potbelly, and Roti. As we ate, we fed both our stomachs and our souls with hearty food and genuine curiosity about each other's lives. Each day, our gang would walk the agency's halls to see who would like to join us for these daily lunches where anything was game for discussion—except work. We went by code names and aliases for fun: PK, Hot Dog, and Dr. J. I was Jenny from the Block, or JFTB for short. Over time, our lunch group became known as the Founders Club because most of our colleagues ate at their desks before we arrived.

My mind was stretched each day, both personally and professionally, and I started to feel like *maybe* I could be okay adjusting to life in a new city. As we got to know each other more deeply at these lunches, beyond our job titles of economist, academic, or auditor, it seemed like we cared about each other as humans. Most of us had just moved to the DC area, and it was our first time working for the government. It felt like a college experience where we were all starting together, which added to our natural bond.

I realized we were growing into more than just friendly colleagues when I had to cancel my Christmas plans to visit family after contracting the flu. PK and Hot Dog "borrowed" the office Christmas tree and brought it to me, along with chicken soup and Chipotle, to make me feel better. It felt both sweet and unfamiliar to lean on others and have support from a group of peers and friends. I wasn't used to that. I'd always taken care of others, whether in my family, in a relationship, or on my own. I began to realize that maybe I didn't have to do that anymore. There were other ways to live.

"Does anyone have any exciting weekend plans?" I asked the Founders Club at lunch one Friday in early fall.

"No, but I was thinking of exploring a swing dance class since it's one of my favorite dance styles," Dr. J offered casually, slowly sipping her tall glass of sparkling water.

"Wait a minute, Dr. J. You *dance*? How am I just now finding out about this?" I couldn't believe that after so many daily lunches together, I was only just discovering that my colleague was a dancer.

"It was something I did a long time ago. Actually, I hadn't even thought about it until you started mentioning you've been wanting to explore the dance scene," Dr. J casually replied.

"Okay, we must go together. Will you be my wing woman for a social dance party this weekend near my house in Bethesda? I'm not brave enough to go alone." *Please, pretty please*, I wanted to add, but I didn't want to seem desperate. This could be my chance to finally check out the dance parties that teased me each week as I walked by the dance studios on my commute home from the metro.

"Okay, sure. I'll do it if you will." Dr. J didn't seem as convinced as I was, but I appreciated her willingness to try.

20

An Invitation
to Dance

A few weeks later, Dr. J and I headed to one of the small dance studios around the corner from my apartment. It was located on the second floor of a busy commercial building, right above a nail salon. The dance floor itself was long and narrow with popcorn ceilings so low I could touch them if I really tried. On this particular Friday night, the energy in the studio was electric, with the lights turned low and the DJ blending contemporary into classic tunes. I was thankful to have my colleague with me as I took my first steps into this new dance community. While I had been taking private lessons with the instructors, I hadn't yet connected with other dancers or made any dance friends.

As I paid my admission fee at check-in, I glanced around the room, trying to avoid making too much eye contact. I was still getting my bearings and wasn't ready to start dancing right away. The dance floor was filled with dancers of different ages, shapes, sizes, and skill levels, though most appeared to be middle-aged. Dr. J and I found a table near the side of the dance floor and settled into our chairs, content to observe for a while. We watched as the other dancers made their way around the small dance floor and embraced after each dance. The studio seemed to be a tight-knit group, and I wasn't sure we belonged.

An Invitation to Dance

As I strapped on my Latin dance shoes, I was invited to the dance floor by the studio owner, an energetic middle-aged gentleman with a strong Australian accent. While I was slightly taller than him, he was strong both physically and in personality, and I found myself smiling throughout the dance, my playful side emerging. I appreciated the gesture and the kind welcome to the social dance party. After that first dance, I spent the evening in mostly unremarkable dances with most of the gentlemen in attendance. Dr. J joined in for a few dances, mostly East Coast Swings, and otherwise watched from the sidelines as I navigated a mix of fast salsa, slow waltz, and sensual bachata that brought back wistful memories of Santos.

Near the end of the night, a tall man approached me from the side. "Hi. I'm Gable." He introduced himself in an accent I couldn't quite place. "Would you like to dance?" he asked, already extending his hand to me in invitation. He seemed both nervous and confident, as if he had been waiting for this specific dance to ask me to join him.

I had noticed Gable when we first walked in, and there was something about him that piqued my interest. "Sure." My cheeks flushed as I accepted his hand and followed him. I hadn't been paying much attention to the music until we made our way to the center of the dance floor. I allowed my body to catch up and was pleasantly surprised to find that the DJ was spinning hustle music.

When I'd lived in New York, the hustle had quickly become one of my favorite dances. I loved the contemporary music, the fast-paced beat, the spins, and the flirty moves. I seized the opportunity to play with lots of creative flair as I danced with Gable.

And one, two, three, and one two three, I silently whispered as we started to connect on the dance floor.

Through my experience dancing in New York and across the globe, I'd learned that you could tell a lot about a person from dancing with them. Character is hard to hide when you're cheek to cheek. I had started using dance to assess my partners and better understand the person behind the moves.

Gable briefly locked eyes with me as we held hands near the center of the floor. Though he was a bit reserved at first, his gentle smile made me sense that he was kind. We were about the same height, but Gable's glorious, full-bodied dark brown hair added an extra inch or so to balance my two-inch black strappy heels.

We started in a slow hustle, moving gently in and out from each other, with both hands often clasped together, swinging around the dance floor. Gable would bring me toward him, gently caressing the small of my back, and then swing me out again as we lifted our free arms with sensual styling. As the music accelerated and our bodies warmed up, I couldn't help but smile.

The music ignited a fire in me, and my confidence soared with each new phrase. Gable shed his reserved demeanor as well, dancing with a captivating smile and understated charm that drew me in. The chemistry between us felt natural and warm, and I didn't want the music to end. In the dimly lit studio, I felt full of light and life. *This is fun*, I thought. As the music slowed, my heart was still racing.

When the song ended and Gable walked me back to my seat, all I could express was a breathless, "Wow. You're a great dancer." He bashfully smiled and made a small bow as he walked away.

I danced with the few remaining gentlemen whom I hadn't danced with yet. All the while, I couldn't get that hustle with Gable out of my mind. It had felt so freeing and fun to share my favorite dance with a partner who was so kind and attentive. I hadn't felt like he was trying to pick me up or hit on me. Our connection on the floor had seemed like it was genuinely fueled by a shared love of dance. I looked forward to dancing with Gable again and learning more about him if I could.

"You ready to head home?" Dr. J asked as the dance party came to a close.

"I am," I said, noticing that Gable was already heading out the door.

Dr. J and I exited the steamy confines of the tiny dance studio and stepped into a brisk autumn night.

"So, what did you think?" Dr. J asked as we made our way back to my apartment.

"Well, it was really nice. Thanks so much for coming with me. I really appreciated the support. I have to say, that hustle with Gable left quite an impression on me." I was surprised at my confession.

"Oh yeah?" Dr. J asked, not surprised in the slightest. "It did seem like the two of you were having a great time. Do you think you'll go back to the dance studio again?"

"Absolutely," I said, already counting the days till the next social dance.

21

Dirty Dancing

As fall faded into winter, I eagerly awaited each Friday night, relishing the chance to immerse myself in the dance studio and see Gable again. With newfound courage, I started to go alone more often. It was liberating to once again express myself in different ways and explore new moves with different partners.

Gable remained a constant each Friday night, always asking me to dance a single hustle and repeatedly leaving me yearning for more. We slowly developed a friendship, stopping for water breaks together and leaving the studio at the same time. There was no pressure for romance, which I appreciated as I wasn't sure I was ready to date again. I wanted to wait at least six more months so I could enjoy being single. I figured that being on my own for almost a year after moving to DC would allow me enough time to reset from the heartbreak of past relationships. Gable's respectful demeanor and gentle spirit were a welcome relief.

One Friday night, Gable sat with me for a while after we danced.

"Hey, I want to show you something." He grabbed his phone and scrolled to a song called "Rather Be."

"Have you listened to this? It's a phenomenal hustle song with beautiful lyrics." He offered me his phone so I could see the album cover.

"No, I haven't. But I will definitely check it out." I wrote the song title in my phone notes and planned to check it out later.

"Have you ever thought about joining the studio performance team?" Gable continued, uncharacteristically chatty. "I've been a member for a few years, and I think you would enjoy it." He looked away, a shy expression on his face as he made this invitation.

"Performance team? I didn't know the studio had one. That sounds amazing. I've learned that I love to perform but not necessarily compete, so that sounds right up my alley." I was excited to learn more.

Gable seemed pleased with my response as he offered a gentle smile. "Great! We meet once a week. You should come and check it out." He looked me in the eyes this time, seeming to tap into the depths of my soul as he offered another gentle smile.

"Sure, I will. But only if you'll be my dance partner," I said, taking the opportunity to flirt in return, hoping he didn't already have a steady partner in the performance group.

"Uh, okay," he replied, seeming flustered by my suggestion and returning to the dance floor to ask another woman to dance.

I sat alone for a few minutes, lost in my thoughts. I wondered if Gable was interested in anything more than friendship. Regardless of his intentions, I thought it was a nice gesture to include me in the performance team. I felt happy to have an opportunity to meet new friends and make the DC area feel more like home. I was ready to give this a shot.

The next Wednesday, I was ready to impress when I joined the performance team rehearsal. As I surveyed the room, I noticed Gable was already practicing some moves in the corner. Our eyes met briefly, and my cheeks flushed. I had enjoyed dancing the hustle with him, but now we were in for something new.

"Okay, class, welcome to our performance team. This season,

we'll be learning a classic mambo from a very famous movie, *Dirty Dancing*," our dance instructor, Rosalie, announced.

Dirty Dancing? That seems a bit risqué. I felt a little nervous to expose my sensual side in front of Gable and this group of dancers I didn't know very well.

Before I knew it, Rosalie was lining up the dancers she thought would make the best partners for our group performance.

"Jennifer, why don't you and Gable dance together? You'd make a good team." She put us next to each other and we both smiled, equal parts delighted and bashful at this pairing.

Rosalie had quickly become one of my favorite dance instructors. She oozed even more sassiness than I did, and she knew I loved to perform, so she always pushed me to be my best. I had mentioned to her before that Gable and I had natural chemistry when we danced the hustle. She clearly had taken note since she paired us up without hesitation.

The performance workshop was scheduled for two months, with a dance showcase right before Valentine's Day. I'd have two months to spend time with Gable and get to know him better. *Will our flirtatious dance moves evolve into something more?* I wasn't sure what I wanted to happen with Gable, but I was happy I'd have a chance to find out.

Gable and I met for an hour before each weekly lesson so we could practice what we were learning. I was happy for the practice, but really, I wanted to spend more time with him and found myself looking forward to these practice sessions even more than the regular rehearsals. Each week, I set an intention to ask a few questions so I could learn more about him. I was curious about the man who had captured my attention with his gentle smile and charming personality. Through our conversations, I learned that Gable had grown up in Brazil and moved to the US in his mid-twenties to pursue his PhD. Coincidentally, we'd both spent our early adult years in Southern California, which gave us more common ground to bond over. He was a scientist, which impressed me, and I could see the passion in his eyes as he spoke about it. He was the first in his family to move away from home and, like me, found solace in dance, which served as a home away from home.

One day, during a particularly engaging conversation, I found the courage to ask, "Do you have any kids?"

"No, but I love them. I would love to have a family." Gable looked at me with a warm smile. Never married, he had been single for the last decade. He spoke a bit wistfully, as if he wasn't sure whether realizing that dream was still possible.

For a moment, I found myself imagining what it would be like to start a family with him. But I pushed those thoughts aside, not wanting to get ahead of myself—after all, we were barely friends off the dance floor. I knew Gable was older than me, but I wasn't sure exactly how much older. It didn't matter to me since I had dated men of all different ages in New York. But I found it interesting that he'd never married since he seemed like such a nice person. I was curious to find out more about his past relationships, but I didn't want to pry. I decided to let things unfold naturally.

After a month of dance practice, Gable and I had developed a light and easy friendship. I felt comfortable around him and found I could be myself without any pressure. During practice one day, I decided to take things up a notch to see if there might be more beneath the surface.

"Hey, Gable! You ready to dance?" I called out as we prepped for practice.

"Of course," he replied, eager to get started.

"Okay, let's go!" With a playful smile, I took off my sweatshirt, revealing a body-hugging T-shirt that said "I'm Your Captain" across the front. It was my first flirtatious gesture, a test to see if he would catch on.

Gable blushed and looked away, trying to hide his laughter.

"You know, the eyes are a window to the soul," I said as I gazed directly into him.

"Yeah, they're dangerous," he replied, still trying to look away.

"I know. That's why we need to keep our gaze connected." I allowed myself to stay vulnerable and waited for his reaction.

Gable seemed surprised by my response, perhaps a bit nervous to unlock that side of himself. I continued to flirt, and we embraced in the classic Patrick Swayze and Jennifer Grey *Dirty Dancing* pose. As he swung me out into a sensual mambo, his hand gently caressed my arm. I kept my gaze locked on him, and for once, he didn't look away. We embodied our roles as we moved through each motion of the routine, our hips delicately moving in a fiery unison of figure eights. We were on fire. As the practice came to a close, I was overheating, my tomato-red cheeks a telltale sign I had pushed my cardio to its limits.

"Here, come with me," Gable suggested, suddenly taking charge and gently gliding me to an open window so I could cool down.

The cold breeze made its way over to me, settling my heart rate and easing the flush in my cheeks. I took a moment to pause at the significance of this simple gesture. Gable's awareness of my needs and his quick, thoughtful response touched me deeply. I was blown away by feeling seen and supported in a new way. I remembered Morey's reaction when I was red-faced after ballet class and how it had shamed me into not dancing again for over a decade. This was truly different.

I appreciated Gable's gentleness and the caution he expressed in caring for me at that moment. It was heartwarming, especially after I'd spent so much time learning about myself and what I wanted in a partner during the last few years. I was beginning to feel there could be something more with Gable. He wasn't looking for a way to control me or make me feel like less than who I was. Nor did he leave me feeling disconnected. He embraced me as I was and celebrated me in full glory, even as a friend.

By late January, the showcase was just around the corner and Gable and I were enjoying one of our last private rehearsals together. We were perfecting our dance moves and getting ready to highlight our sensual mambo. During our warm-up, he asked, "Hey, what are you up to this weekend?"

Without hesitation, I replied, "I was thinking of checking out the Washington National Cathedral. I haven't been there yet, and they have a Sunday service that looks amazing."

"Oh, nice. I love that place. It's beautiful," Gable replied.

Before I could think twice, I surprised myself by asking, "Why don't you join me?" Just as suddenly, I realized Gable might interpret this as a date since we hadn't spent much time together outside of practice.

"Really? Okay. I'll think about it," Gable said, looking both surprised and excited by my proposal. It was hard to read his facial expression, but I found myself hoping he'd come.

When Sunday arrived, I made my way to the middle section of the nave and looked up, awed by the cathedral's splendor. The neo-Gothic church, resplendent with stained glass, recalled my European adventures, especially traveling to Paris. I turned and saw a beautiful circular stained-glass window behind me. Light shone through what looked like a hundred red and pink flower petals, and I caught my breath.

I returned my gaze to the front of the church as the organ swelled to announce the start of the service. Looking around, I searched for Gable, but he was nowhere to be seen. Earlier, he had texted to assure me that he was coming, and I felt nervous waiting for him. It had been years since I attended a formal church service. As a teenager, the church was an extension of myself, but that particular experience had left me feeling too controlled and constrained. I was looking forward to experiencing a traditional church service and appreciated that the cathedral welcomed everyone regardless of their spiritual beliefs. I embraced the freedom associated with this inclusive environment, and it reopened my heart to my spiritual beliefs, helping me recognize that the controlling way I'd experienced the church during my youth wasn't the only way to get close to God. As I started to sing the first hymn, there was a gentle tap on my shoulder. It was Gable.

"Hi there," I whispered, offering him a quick hug. "So glad you made it."

"Me too," he replied, smiling warmly and holding my gaze. He was dressed casually in jeans and a sweater, and he smelled of fresh cologne.

This was starting to feel like a pseudo-date, but I didn't want to overthink it. As the music continued, we shared a single program, leaning our heads together, cheek to cheek, so we could follow the program as instructed. When the pastor welcomed the congregation and gave us a moment to greet each other with peace, Gable leaned over and kissed me gently on the cheek. "Peace be with you," he whispered.

"Peace be with you," I replied, blushing at this intimate gesture.

As the service ended and the organ swelled for the postlude, Gable and I made our way to the Bishop's Garden behind the church. We found an empty wooden bench that reminded me of the garden I'd encountered in London's Notting Hill so many years ago.

"Thanks again for inviting me. I had a really great time. I love it here," Gable said as we took in the sweet vista surrounding us.

I wasn't sure if Gable was religious, but I agreed that the cathedral was a magical oasis in the city. "My pleasure," I said.

"I'm glad you came. It's beautiful here." I took a deep breath and relished the peal of church bells in the background.

We continued to talk and get to know each other better. As we spoke, I felt myself being drawn to Gable. He had a way of making me feel comfortable and at ease, yet he still sparked my heart.

"Uh, I have a question I want to ask you, but I am afraid." Gable shifted nervously in his seat, and I could see hesitation in his eyes.

A sudden jolt of anxiety shot through me. *Is he going to tell me he's married or in a relationship? Not interested in women?* I realized that I was having feelings for Gable, and my mind started to race as I waited for him to drop whatever this question was.

Finally, he spoke. "Do you know how old I am?"

I let out a sigh of relief. "How old you are? Yes. I googled you," I admitted, unscathed by our nineteen-year age difference. I confessed that I had done a little research on this mystery man and had stumbled upon our age difference in one of my searches. Now I felt like we really *were* on a first date.

"You did?" Gable looked surprised.

"Yes. Honestly, the age difference doesn't bother me. We have a great connection and seem to have similar beliefs and core values. I've really appreciated the way you're so caring and thoughtful as a dance partner, and I feel like I can be myself with you. That means a lot to me." I hoped he could feel the sincerity in my words, but wondered if I was saying too much. This felt like more than two dancers meeting as friends.

Gable flashed a warm smile. "Wow. Okay. Honestly, that's a big relief. I really enjoyed our time dancing together, too, but I was afraid you wouldn't want to hang out if you knew how old I was. Thank you for being so great." He leaned in and we settled into a warm, intimate hug.

Our non-date had taken an interesting turn, and I wondered

if this was the start of something more. *Maybe he thinks this is a date, too. Have we just crossed over the line from friendship?* I closed my eyes and let the peaceful chiming of church bells wash over me. I realized Gable ticked all the boxes that really mattered to me. Despite the age gap, I felt an undeniable connection between us, and not one that had happened overnight. It had been built over time in many small ways. As I reflected on our time practicing dance together over the last few months, I saw that Gable had been there for me in a way no romantic partner ever had. His steady and patient approach had a calming effect on me, and I was drawn to his quiet good humor and strength. He seemed willing to play the long game, and that was something I hadn't encountered before. As I opened my eyes, I stole a quick glance at Gable, who was lost in thought, gazing out into the Bishop's Garden. *Were we both starting to see each other in a new light?*

22

Soul Equal

In the final weeks leading up to our performance, Gable and I continued to rehearse, avoiding any mention of our encounter at the cathedral. We seemed comfortable staying in the friend zone, but I still wondered if there might be more to our connection.

After practice one day, Gable asked if I had ever thought about taking West Coast Swing classes. I had seen some dances in New York, but I'd never had a chance to take lessons. I'd always admired the swing dancers who gracefully moved in and out from each other like a rubber band extending and compressing along a train track. The dance style particularly appealed to me since it allowed for tremendous creativity and improvisation, a freedom that I loved in my own dance explorations. Gable suggested a nearby studio that had just started a weekly West Coast Swing class and invited me to check it out with him.

"Sure! I'd love that. The only problem is that I don't have a car. I don't think that studio is metro-accessible." I felt defeated; I hadn't figured out the area's car services yet.

Without hesitation, Gable offered to pick me up.

"Okay," I said. "Let's do it." I was excited about this possibility. Plus, the drive would give us more time to get to know each other off the dance floor—the suburban studios hadn't afforded the casual opportunity to grab a post-dance coffee or dinner like the studios in New York had. I wondered if Gable just wanted a familiar partner to dance with or if there was more behind his invitation. I was determined to explore the potential between us before our dance performance class ended.

For the next couple of weeks, Gable picked me up outside my apartment promptly at 8:00 p.m. Before each fifteen-minute drive, I planned which questions I wanted to ask so I could probe a little deeper and peel away his layers. I wanted to learn more about his values, his past relationships, and how he wanted to live his life.

"Gable, what's important to you in a relationship?" I asked one evening a few days before our *Dirty Dancing* performance, ready to cut to the chase.

"Wow. That's a bold question." He laughed, surprised by my directness as he thought about how to respond. Then he continued, "Well, I've learned in my past relationships that it's critical to find the balance between togetherness and independence. I want to share a life with someone who has their own passions and takes time to embrace them. It's important to maintain your sense of self in a relationship, and I've found that can be difficult to achieve."

"Yes, it's so true. Trying to be interdependent is such a key challenge, and it's not easy to keep a sense of freedom and individuality while also integrating your life with someone. I haven't experienced that yet either," I replied, wondering where the conversation might lead us.

With each drive and chat, we shared more and more of our values. It soon became clear that we shared a desire to live a life full of adventure, family, and dance. As we got to know each other, each small journey added to my understanding of Gable, and I realized I was starting to fall for him.

On the day before our debut *Dirty Dancing* performance, we were enjoying our weekly West Coast Swing class. We both felt confident in our basic moves and took turns dancing with many partners at the practice party that evening. We joked and laughed, and a playful vibe filled the air between us until the final song came on and Gable invited me to dance. I joined him, not thinking much of it since we were now so comfortable dancing together. But something about that dance felt different. Intimacy had been bubbling below the surface, and Gable seemed to have left any inhibition or caution at the dance studio entrance. He looked me in the eyes, his gaze flirting with desire as our bodies moved in unison back and forth across the dance floor. Despite only knowing a few basic moves, our chemistry was electric, and the passion of the dance melted us into each other. My heart raced and butterflies exploded in my stomach as the song ended and Gable hugged me tightly. On the drive home, my mind couldn't stop racing. Something had shifted between us, and I wondered if Gable could be the one. *Is this my person?* I wondered. My heart was yearning to shout a resounding *yes!!!*

On the ride home, Gable asked me, "What are you doing next weekend?"

"You mean, on Valentine's Day?" I teased, wanting to know if this was going to be an official date.

"Yes. There's a dance at the Italian embassy. Would you like to come with me?" he continued.

"You mean, like a real date?" I asked, wanting to be sure of his intentions.

Gable laughed and replied sweetly, "Um, yeah. If that's okay." I could tell it had taken a lot of courage for him to answer that question.

"I would love to," I said, thrilled to have a date with Gable for Valentine's Day.

As we approached my apartment, I held Gable for an extra beat as we gave each other a warm hug goodbye and I headed inside, not quite ready to call it a night. About thirty minutes later, I opened my computer and checked my email. There was a note from Gable at the top of my inbox with the subject line "Soul Equal." I was intrigued.

Gable had attached an article to his message, and it discussed the concept of a "soul equal" as opposed to a soul mate. The article proposed that the best kind of romantic love occurs when both partners feel free to be themselves, maintaining interdependence and creating a high level of energy between them. The description seemed to perfectly describe how I had felt when I danced with Gable that night. *Maybe he felt it too.*

As I scanned the article, my heart raced and warm tingles found their way through my spine. The article highlighted what I'd been feeling for Gable but hadn't been able to put into words. From the outside, it might have seemed like we weren't a match given our significant age difference. And yet, when you find your soul equal, societal norms don't matter. I recognized the beauty of feeling completely myself when I was with him, and our energy together was full of passion. I immediately responded to Gable's email with a text. He needed to know how I felt.

Wow, what an interesting article. I can definitely relate, I wrote.

Oh yeah? How so? I could sense he was still being cautious.

Well, didn't you feel our chemistry tonight? It was off the charts!! And can't you see that I am flirting with you? I decided to be more direct. It was time to put my heart and cards on the table.

You are? Even through text, I could feel his surprise.

Yes!!! I replied eagerly, hoping he finally got the message.

Wow, I thought you might be, but I wasn't so sure. And I didn't want to risk our friendship, so I wasn't going to make a move. But I'd love to explore something more, he finally offered.

It was amazing to at last expand our relationship and share our feelings for one another. We exchanged sweet and flirtatious texts back and forth for a few hours before we finally called it a night. We had a performance to get through the next day, and it was already after midnight.

The next evening, the moment finally arrived for us to share our *Dirty Dancing* performance with our beloved community. I was both excited and nervous for our debut, feeling there was much more at stake now than when we'd first started practicing together. Gable suggested we meet for a drink before the show, and I eagerly agreed. I arrived at the restaurant next to my apartment before he did. I took a seat at the bar and ordered a dirty martini. A jazz musician played in the background, enhancing the sophisticated and romantic air. When Gable came in a few minutes after me, my heart skipped a beat.

"What are you drinking?" he asked nervously.

"A very dirty martini," I replied, popping the olive in my mouth with a sly smile.

He laughed. "One for me, too, please," he said to the bartender.

"I've never had one before," he confided to me.

"They're dangerous," I archly flirted.

"Oh, wow—that's strong," Gable said after his drink arrived and he took the first sip. He seemed out of his league as he placed his martini back on the bar.

"Yes, it is." I laughed. We weren't big drinkers, and the alcohol hit us both a bit too hard, especially in light of our upcoming dance performance. With a mix of awkwardness and playfulness, we leaned into each other for a hug. It was our first real date since expressing our mutual interest the night before, and we were both unsure of how to proceed.

"Let's get to the dance," Gable suggested, placing his half-full glass back on the bar. I tossed back the rest of my drink and took his hand as we made our way to the studio. It was cold outside, and I relished the warmth of his hand in mine. He gently squeezed mine as we entered the small dance studio.

"Come here for a second," he whispered, leading me into a hallway where no one could see us. He approached me slowly and gave me a soft kiss on the lips. My spine tingled and there were butterflies in my belly. I kissed him back. The passion deepened, and I didn't want this magical kiss to end. It felt like we were two teenagers sneaking around in a hallway, and I enjoyed this playful side of our connection. *This is my person*, I thought. Gable gently pulled away and we locked eyes before walking into the dance studio together, trying to hide the obvious detour we had just taken.

The next hour flew by in a blur as we made our way through our *Dirty Dancing* routine. As the music started, Gable stared at me all googly-eyed while my heart melted at his gaze. We embraced our sexy, flirty roles knowing there was something deeper between us that the audience could not see. Working together on this dance had been our opportunity to move slowly and to find each other over time. Now, in this moment, it felt like we were meant to be together all along.

As our group performance came to an end, Gable whispered in my ear, "I have a surprise for you."

The music changed and Gable grabbed me by the hand, leading me to the dance floor. We were the only people on the floor, and the audience clapped in anticipation.

"Let's welcome Gable and Jennifer," the DJ announced over the applause.

I wasn't sure what was happening as I heard the familiar sound of a tango, but with a slow, unfamiliar beat. Gable pulled me into a close embrace as we made our way across the floor, fully intertwined. And then I heard it—the lyrics of the song "Rather Be," the song Gable had shared with me six months earlier after one of our first dances together. For the first time, I listened attentively to the lyrics. It was a love song about finally finding your perfect match. I wondered, *Was Gable interested in me from the beginning? Was it love at first sight for him?* Did it even matter? We were here together now.

After exploring my passions and testing various partners on and off the dance floor over the last four years, it had become clear which energy and light I was drawn to. I had grown more trusting of my own inner wisdom, and I had finally found the courage to honor it. I was no longer tied to a life of forced and rigid choreography; I knew what I was looking for and what felt right for me. I wrapped my arms around Gable and our foreheads touched. We breathed as one, and our souls communicated without words. There was a lightness about me, like my feet were floating off the ground, as I listened to Gable speak with the clear forward motion of his stance and torso, asking me with his gentle lead if I would like to follow.

The music shifted into a hustle beat and Gable glided me out, offering me an opportunity to bring out my sassiness and style in full form. As we danced, I realized that things in my life would never be the same. This dance was more than just a performance. It was a declaration of love, the moment when we finally found each other.

Epilogue

Three months after our first date, Gable and I returned to the Washington National Cathedral together, the place where it all began. There in the Bishop's Garden, I felt a gentle touch on the small of my back and turned to see Gable standing beside me. Our hearts racing, bodies connected, we closed our eyes, and the world disappeared as we glided together in a graceful tango. Dancing in silence with only the church bells to accompany us, we were tuned to the same silent inner rhythm, both mesmerized by the beauty around us and the glory of our intimate embrace. As we danced to the pealing bells, Gable slowly pulled away from me. As I turned to face him, he was down on one knee.

Acknowledgments

Writing this memoir was at least ten years in the making. The first three pages of the journal I bought after moving to New York City in 2011 were filled with the outline of the book I wanted to write one day. That book looked very different from the memoir you just read, but nonetheless, my story was longing to be written.

They say when you write a memoir, the memoir that wants to be written will emerge and you need to follow the path. It's not always easy to chart that path from the onset and my story is a testament to this. It was a winding path of refining and carving away the pieces that weren't necessary to illustrate the freedom that I found through my adventures to find my voice. And there were so many people who made this dream possible.

Thank you to my dear friend Lori Mihalich-Levin for introducing me to Brooke Warner and Linda Joy Myers's memoir writing program and to Lori Lothian for reminding me that becoming a published author was part of my destiny. Those experiences set the trajectory for me to make this published memoir a reality. Thanks to Linda Joy for your guidance and wisdom throughout this process and Brooke in creating a sisterhood that is She Writes Press.

Thank you to Ellen Mendlow for helping me filter down thirty-five years of experience into a cohesive theme while maintaining my authentic voice through the developmental edit. Thanks to my early readers Rachel, Meg, Colleen, Kim, Kathryn,

Dana, Chris, Erica, Judy, and many more who provided encouragement and enthusiasm for the story I was telling. Thanks to my mom for reading nearly every version of the multiple manuscripts and for being willing to endure repeatedly the challenging experiences and provide constructive feedback along the way.

Thank you to my husband for being there for me each day and allowing me to hide away when inspiration struck so that I could complete this manuscript in less than a year. Your unconditional support means more than you know.

To my daughter, may you always seek adventure, stretch yourself beyond your limits, and be strong in trusting your own voice.

And to my readers, thank you for sharing this journey with me and I hope you find the courage to say yes to where your intuition guides you. For the world needs who you were made to be.

About the Author

Jenn Todling is an author, speaker, executive coach, as well as an adjunct instructor at the University of Denver as part of its Frontline Manager Leadership Program. Formerly an audit partner at a global Big 4 accounting firm with over twenty years of professional services experience and an ICF-certified transformational leadership coach for over ten years, Jenn helps her clients express their soul in their work and life. A lover of adventure, travel, and dance, she currently resides near her hometown of Boulder, Colorado, with her husband (and dance partner) and daughter. *Dancing on My Own Two Feet* is her first book. Learn more at jenntodling.com.

Looking for your next great read?

We can help!

Visit www.shewritespress.com/next-read
or scan the QR code below for a list
of our recommended titles.

She Writes Press is an award-winning
independent publishing company founded to
serve women writers everywhere.